Jonathan Wild

Conman and
Cutpurse

Jonathan Wild

Conman and Cutpurse

JOHN VAN DER KISTE

AMBERLEY

First published 2009

Amberley Publishing
Cirencester Road, Chalford,
Stroud, Gloucestershire, GL6 8PE

www.amberley-books.com

British Library Cataloguing in Publication Data.
A catalogue record for this book is available from the British Library.

ISBN 978 1 84868 219 1

Typesetting and origination by Amberley Publishing
Printed in Great Britain

Contents

List of Illustrations

Acknowledgements

I would like to thank my wife Kim for her tireless encouragement, support, and reading through of the draft manuscript; and to Sarah Flight and James Pople at Amberley Publishing for their hard work.

A highwayman

CHAPTER ONE

Wild's Early Life

Jonathan Wild was not only the most famous criminal in London of the eighteenth century, but probably the most famous in Britain of his time. Known to posterity as the 'Director of a Corporation of Thieves', or as 'the Prince of Robbers', he made a remarkably successful living out of running a gang of thieves, while posing as a thief-taker or unofficial policeman. In retrospect he was the one of the first and most famous racketeers, although the word did not come into common usage for another two centuries. One of his biographers, Gerald Howson, has described him as 'the first modern gangster', a precursor of Al Capone, and compared the London of the 1720s to the Chicago of the 1920s. At the same time, he brilliantly exploited the contemporary press, and the fears of the nation, making himself something of a public hero during his lifetime. Only when towards the end of his days, once he was exposed for the self-serving duplicitous mastermind he had always been, and sent to the gallows, did the general public admiration turn to contempt.

Wild was born at Wolverhampton, the eldest of five children, and baptised in St Peter's Church on 6 May 1683. His parents were reputedly 'mean but honest'; his father was a carpenter and joiner who died about 1699, and his mother was a fruit seller in Wolverhampton market, who died about 1721. One brother, John, became a bailiff and town crier of Wolverhampton, but his fierce espousal of the Jacobite cause proved his undoing. During the rebellion of 1715 when it was thought that the Old Pretender might arrive in the town, he was the ringleader of a group who climbed on to the roof of the Presbyterian Meeting House, St John's Street, toasted the good health of 'His Majesty King James III', and incited the mob to wreck the building. He then led the motley gang to West Bromwich and destroyed the Meeting House there as well. For this he was publicly flogged, imprisoned for two years, and died in 1720. The other brother, Andrew, was said to be a petty criminal. Of the sisters, one married a bucklemaker, the other a combmaker.

Jonathan, who in time would prove even less law-abiding than his brothers, attended day school in St John's Lane and received a general education in reading, writing and accounts, in the hope that it would qualify him for a life in business. His father had planned that he would follow the family tradition of becoming a carpenter, but then at the age of fifteen apprenticed him for seven years to a bucklemaker in Birmingham. At the end of this period he returned to Wolverhampton to pursue this trade. In April 1701 he married, and he and his wife had a son. Many details of his early life are disputed, and some are thought to have been invented by biographers for the sake of filling out a story where facts were lacking. It has however been suggested that he first travelled to London in 1704 as servant to a lawyer, Councillor Daniel, but he either absconded or was dismissed for misconduct. After that he became a setter to bailiffs (hunting out debtors so that his employers could arrest them) attached to Marshalsea Court, Clifford's Inn, Holborn.

It was related that one day shortly before leaving Wolverhampton he borrowed a horse, took it to London and sold it. Once he had found his employment as a setter less profitable and more dangerous than bucklemaking, he returned home. The owner of the animal allowed him to pay back its value by instalments. After he had paid the second instalment, he refused to reimburse any further. By not doing so any more, he declared, he broke the articles of his contract, and articles once thus broken could not be said to subsist, so were no longer binding. Here was a man who would never be short on ideas as to making money, by fair means or foul.

Becoming bored with life in Wolverhampton, he returned to London, leaving his wife and child to fend for themselves. At first he continued to work at bucklemaking, but within a few months his extravagance and love of good living got him deeply into debt. In March 1710 he was arrested and sentenced to four years in Wood Street Compter, one of the main debtors' prisons. Prisons were notoriously corrupt, with gaolers always ready to demand a bribe, or 'garnish', for any minor comfort. While he was in prison, he had every opportunity to associate with the cream of London's criminal underclass. Hearing of their exploits and ways of making easy money on the wrong side of the law appealed to him more than the idea of pursuing an honest but humble trade as his parents had done. In a pamphlet which he wrote a few years later, he recalled that during this period of imprisonment 'it was impossible but he must, in some measure, be let into the secrets of the criminals there under confinement, and particularly Mr Hitchen's management.'

Charles Hitchen was his original mentor. Born in London about 1675 of a poor family, he was a former cabinet-maker. In 1703 he married Elizabeth Wells, and they lived in a house on the north side of St Paul's Churchyard. Elizabeth inherited property from her father when he died in 1711, which she was persuaded to sell by her husband, thus enabling him to purchase the office of Under-Marshal of the City for £700 in the following year. It was the duty and the privilege of the two City marshals, with a small force of six men, to carry out policing duties that centred principally on keeping the streets of London clear of vagrants, prostitutes, and unlicensed traders. Fees accruing from this and other work carried out at the behest of the Lord Mayor, as well as an annual salary and allowances of about £100, soon repaid the purchase price of the office. In the early seventeenth century, over a hundred years before the establishment of the metropolitan police force, London depended on localised policing. The maintenance of law and order was left to a number of constables and 'peace officers' of the crown, a few independent bodies of men who rarely cooperated with and generally obstructed each other.

Many of them, like Hitchen himself, were involved in crime themselves to some extent. In 1712 he admitted that he personally knew about two thousand people within the 'Bills of Mortality', or the 109 parishes covering parts of central and east London, who made their living solely through theft. It was widely thought that this number had doubled by around 1720, and that professional thieves in the City of London and Westminster alone, both full-time and part-time, numbered between 10,000 and 12,000. He had always been ready to exploit the opportunities involving corruption that the authority of the marshal's office afforded its holder, and shamelessly abused his position by practising extortion on an extravagant scale from thieves and from their potential victims. His methods included accepting bribes to let thieves out of jail, selectively arresting criminals, and coercing sexual services from molly houses, or homosexual brothels. Soon after assuming office he began to extort protection money from brothel- and tavern-keepers, and used his powers of arrest to threaten young pickpockets with prosecution, not to discourage them from thieving but to coerce them into bringing him the goods that they stole, so he could negotiate with their victims for the return of their belongings for a fee.

Such thief-takers, acting as middlemen between thieves and their victims, were well known in the reign of Queen Anne, and their activities were increasing because of efforts made by Parliament and the City magistrates to catch and punish receivers of stolen goods. It was generally safer and more profitable for thieves to return the items they stole for a portion of their value. Many of their victims were willing to pay to recover their goods, particularly merchants and tradesmen who lost pocketbooks and valuable commercial papers to pickpockets and other thieves. Hitchen had probably already begun his involvement in helping to arrange such transactions before he invested his wife's money in the office of under-marshal.

Another reason for the dramatic rise of crime in London over the previous thirty years or so, with property crime in particular, was London's growing importance as a centre of commerce. With the growth in usage of paper money transfers, the early draft notices, and 'notes of hand', or agreements to pay the bearer, pickpockets were causing larger economic losses to traders and merchants. The publication of daily newspapers had led to a rising interest in crime and criminals, and as they reported on the subject, the public became ever more interested in the issues of criminals and policing. Everyone was repelled but fascinated by colourful criminals, some of them celebrated as loveable rogues, and while they might have a guilty interest in the escapades of the lawless, they were just as keen to support and place their faith in the valiant crime-fighters who helped to make their lives safer. In the last few decades the city's population had more than doubled, thus making it harder to maintain law and order effectively on a major scale. In 1723 the Black Act was passed, partly in response to an outbreak of poaching committed by men who disguised themselves by blacking their faces. It listed over 350 capital felonies, which included not only the major offences such as wilful murder and treason, but also certain types of malicious damage to private property that were considered as misdemeanours against the public, as opposed to personal wrongs which were civil offences. To an extent this accounted for the statistical increase in crime, reflecting an increase in the number of activities deemed to be criminal; between 1688 and 1820 the number of capital offences rose from about fifty to over two hundred. Hanging crimes included not only murder, rape and sodomy, but also arson, forgery, housebreaking, maiming cattle, and even offences which look comparatively trivial to a later age such as cutting down trees in an avenue, destroying turnpikes and sending threatening letters.

Looked at from one perspective, London saw an alarming rise not only in thieving, but in organised crime during the period. It was rendered less safe when a system of street lighting, devised and financed around 1680 by Edward Hemming, had fallen into disuse since he lost his patent in 1717. Newspapers complained that the streets of London were often in almost total darkness, especially after the hours of daylight in summer, while the lighting tax which ostensibly subsidised the facility had been increased. No man's house, it was said, was safe unless fortified and defended by a small private army of servants, and no man found it safe to drive out by day or night unless he was armed to the teeth with swords, pistols, muskets and blunderbusses. Against this has to be balanced the fact that crimes were better reported than ever before. Barely a day went by without the London press featuring sensational accounts of highway robberies, cold-blooded murders and the like. This had the unfortunate effect of adding romance and drama to a life of crime, and a certain minority of criminals began to pride themselves on carrying out their activities with a bravado that would look rather becoming in print. That the press was apparently prepared to pander to such elements with the oxygen of publicity was possibly not that conducive to law and order.

One of the most effective ways of making money was by becoming a thief-taker. Such an 'occupation' was effectively if inadvertently created by an Act of Parliament passed in 1697, which offered rewards for the capture and successful prosecution of highwaymen. Thief-takers seized criminals and either handed them over to the authorities, or prosecuted them themselves, once they had found that the cash rewards involved offered made them a very good living. Apprehending highwaymen, coiners and burglars brought them £40 each, in addition to any equipment the criminal may have been using, and an additional £100 if the robbery was committed within five miles of Charing Cross. Such remuneration was equivalent to three to four years' wages for most people. These rewards also carried a free pardon for any offences the thief-taker may have committed, and if he died, any reward thus accrued would be passed on to his descendants. In the pre-police force era, offering such gratuities was one of the few ways by which the government could persuade people to assist in law enforcement by helping to catch criminals, and lead to the breaking up of gangs in. However, it also had the unfortunate effect of encouraging corruption, blackmail and perjury. Far from being a precursor of the modern Neighbourhood Watch system, it had the result of causing criminals to turn on each other, creating an atmosphere of mutual suspicion and violence, and encouraging the cleverest to work on both sides of the law.

Hitchen was one of the first to see the financial advantages of acting as a 'finder' of stolen merchandise and negotiating a fee for the return of the stolen items. Once he had the authority of the office behind him he became more active in this sphere. It was not long before he regarded it as legitimate enough to begin boasting shamelessly of controlling dozens of pickpockets and other thieves, which gave him the power to extort money out of tradesmen to prevent them from being robbed, as well as seeking out their victims to put pressure on them to make use of his services as a middleman.

Success and over-confidence soon went to his head, and his tactics became so aggressive that many respectable men in the City complained about him. His testimony on the rise of crime was given during an investigation by the London Board of Aldermen of his activities in September 1712, about ten months after he had taken up the post.

By then they had become wise to his ways, interviewed his accusers and several of the young pickpockets he had been dealing with, relieved him of his duties and suspended him from the office of Under-Marshal in 1713. He was allowed to retain his title and salary, as the aldermen were reluctant to discharge him from an office that he had so recently purchased. To dismiss him altogether would be a devaluation of the post, since the City treasury had benefited from a portion of the sale price which he had originally paid for his employment. He was reinstated in April 1714, largely on the strength of his claim that he was developing a new plan to diminish crime in the City.

In the months that followed the end of the War of the Spanish Succession and the demobilisation of Marlborough's continental army, and the discharge of large numbers of sailors, violent street crime was a pressing issue for the government. During the next few years nobody would be more adept in exploiting the fact than Jonathan Wild.

The trial of a highwayman at the Old Bailey

CHAPTER TWO

Wild and Hitchen

During his suspension Charles Hitchen enlisted Wild to help him keep control of his thieves while he himself was officially sidelined, telling him that he thought it would be as well if he was initiated into some knowledge of the secrets of the criminal underworld. As Wild's experience was inferior to Hitchen's, the latter could teach him a good deal. Although suspended, he still retained the power of acting as constable, and had the ear of the aldermen if not the Lord Mayor, whose trust he had largely forfeited.

While in captivity Wild behaved himself well and soon earned the keepers' confidence. He was granted the 'Liberty of the Gate', allowed out at night to aid in the arrest of thieves, and paid a small amount for errands performed. As he proved himself such a reliable assistant, they appointed him underkeeper to the 'disorderly persons' who were arrested each night and kept in the prison until their cases could be brought before a magistrate.

Among the petty criminals and prostitutes whose acquaintance he cultivated while in captivity was the notorious Mary Milliner, widely regarded as 'one of the most abandoned prostitutes and pickpockets in the town'. She had also been imprisoned for debt, and alongside Hitchen became Wild's ready instructor in the ways of the criminal world. One of her favourite practices was the 'twang', in which the man went out with a 'woman of the town'. Once she had found herself a customer, he would be lurking at a convenient distance, ready to rob him. Sometimes it might be a matter of turning a simple conversation into an argument or sham quarrel, thus creating a diversion so that she could relieve the man of a watch or a purse of guineas and give her an opportunity to get away without being noticed. For a while they did very successfully out of this arrangement.

Through Mary he became well acquainted with various gangs, and the ways in which they carried out their robberies. He learned just where and how they operated, and how they disposed of goods after they came into their possession while still evading the law. Soon he became adept at giving their advice and presenting himself as something of a leader among them, making himself useful and putting his calculating mind at their disposal. At the same time he was smart enough to decline any invitation to go out with them on their escapades.

In 1712 an Act of Parliament for the Relief of Insolvent Debtors was passed, enabling prisoners who because of their custodial sentences were prevented from working in order to discharge their debts, to be freed so they would not become a burden on the nation. It was conditional on all those applying for this pardon to draw up schedules of their assets and remaining debts, and their creditors would have to be content with such payments as could be made from the assets. Wild and Milliner duly took advantage of this to apply for discharge from the Compter in December 1712, and they set up house together (or more likely a brothel) in Lewkenor's Lane, Covent Garden. That Mary Milliner was already married to a waterman in town and Jonathan Wild had a family in Wolverhampton was of no account to either of them. He served as her 'tough' when she went out on the streets at night, while continuing to acquaint himself with the whys and wherefores of the underworld, and his criminal career began in earnest at around this time. At first he made a living from the proceeds of prostitution and from occasional work as a bailiff's assistant, but from that it was a small step to racketeering and acting as a fence or receiver of stolen goods, into which Hitchen had initiated him.

Around spring or early summer 1713 Hitchen approached Wild and asked him to accompany him as an assistant in his nightly 'rambles'. The ostensible objective of these excursions was inspecting disorderly houses with a view to trying to reform them by warning them they risked closure if their activities continued unchecked, but in reality this was merely a cover for extorting protection money from them and finding new opportunities for trafficking in stolen goods.

While Wild was honing his thieving skills, he continued to act as Hitchen's right-hand man. The partners in crime posed as the saviours of society, pretending to try and keep lawless elements under control while ruthlessly exploiting the situation for their own financial benefit. They paraded the City of London streets from Temple Bar to the Minories after darkness, calling in at alehouses and brandy shops, where the hosts were eager to supply these self-proclaimed benefactors with drinks on the house. Hitchen would say little to them, beyond making them understand that he expected them to give him any information they might have of pocket-books, or any goods stolen, as a gratuity for their good works.

To some of the women in one of the shops, Hitchen said it would be to their advantage if they no longer made it a common practice to confide in 'the bullies and rogues' that followed them of their lawless escapades. He personally assured them that the whole lot of them would be turned over to the authorities unless they delivered to him all the pocket-books, watches and similar items which they might acquire in the course of their business. Any refusal to cooperate with him or Wild, 'his man', would result in a sentence at Bridewell, a notorious poorhouse and prison, particularly for 'disorderly women'. Even though Hitchen was under suspension, chiefly for 'not suppressing the practices of such vermin as you' it was still within his power to punish them, and if they did not defer to him they would pay dearly. They also went searching houses of ill-fame, apprehending disorderly and suspected persons, but those who were smart enough to advance them a bribe or two were allowed to carry on their activities undisturbed.

During one of these walks Hitchen suddenly seized two or three pickpockets, reprimanding them for not paying their respects, asking whether they did not see him, and to what part of the town they were going. They answered that they had seen and recognised him at a distance, but he caught hold of them so quickly that they had no time to address him. They had been 'strolling' they said, over Moorfields, and then to the Blue Boar, trying to find him, but as there was no sign of him at first, they thought he might have been indisposed. Hitchen said he had planned to meet them there, but he had been employed the whole day with his 'new man'. He then warned them to be very careful not to oblige any person but myself, or servant, with pocket-books; if they disobeyed him they would 'swing for it', and they were out in the city every night watching out for them. The pickpockets promised faithfully, and went on their way.

A few nights later, as both men were walking together in the direction of St Paul's, Hitchen said to Wild that he would show him a brandy-shop that entertained only whores and thieves. He had been told that a woman of the town who frequented it had just robbed a gentleman of his watch and pocket-book. They would go into this house, and if they could find this woman, he would assume a sterner countenance, wring a confession from her by continued threats, and thus get possession of the watch and pocket-book, while Wild kept her companion's attention occupied. After giving him a description of her, he told Wild to call her, and to say that if she did not find out what had happened to the watch and pocket-book by next day at the latest, she would be sent to the Compter and then to the workhouse.

They then went into the shop to look for the woman, and found her at once. Hitchen looked angrily at her and Wild followed his example. The patrons told them that they looked as sour as two devils, to which Hitchen snapped that he would turn some of them into devils if they did not immediately discover the watch and pocket-book he was employed to find. When some of them innocently told him they did not know what he was talking about, he persisted in more conciliatory fashion that it was extremely ungrateful of them to deny him this small request. Every time, he said, whenever he was let into the secret of anything that was to be taken from a gentleman he always shared the information with them, describing him so precisely that he would be unmistakable; 'and there is so little got at this rate, that the devil may trade with you for me!' Hitchen then nodded to Wild, who called one of the women to the door. She was wise to their schemes, and retorted that Hitchen was an 'Unconscionable devil' who could easily get five or even ten guineas this way, but was too mean to pass on 'as many shillings upon us unfortunate wretches'. However, rather than go to the Compter, she would try and do as they asked.

She then returned to Hitchen, asked him what he would give for the delivery of the watch, which was worth about £8, and the pocket-book, containing several notes and goldsmiths' bills. He told her he would give a guinea, adding that it would be much better for her to comply with him than end up in Newgate, which she undoubtedly would if she refused to cooperate. The woman replied that the watch was in pawn for 40s, and if he did not advance that sum she should be obliged to strip herself for its redemption; though, when her scarf was laid aside 'she had nothing underneath but furniture for a paper-mill'. After further negotiation, he allowed her 30s for the watch and book, which she accepted. Perhaps it is unnecessary to add that the watch was never returned to the owner.

A little while later, a drunken man who was going into the Blue Boar, near Moorfields, with a streetwalker, lost his watch. When he had sobered up he applied to Hitchen for help but Wild, who was familiar enough with the way between Cripplegate and Moorfields, was first to find the woman. Hitchen then seized her and bullied her into confessing that she had stolen the watch and taken it to a woman who kept a brandy-shop nearby, asking her to help her sell it. The mistress of the brandy-shop readily answered that she had it from 'an honest young woman' who regularly came to her house, and whose husband was away at sea. She herself had pawned the watch for its full value.

Meanwhile a watchmaker had purchased the watch for 50s. When this transaction was discovered, Hitchen and his assistants immediately went to the watchmaker's shop, seized the unfortunate man, took him to a public house, and told him that if he did not get it back at once he would be imprisoned in Newgate. Unaccustomed to dealing in suspect goods, the watchmaker insisted that he had bought the merchandise in good faith, and the person who sold it to him would produce the woman that stole it if it had indeed been stolen, as the woman was present at the time. Hitchen replied that he himself had no business with the persons who took the property in the first place, only those in whose possession it was found. If he did not instantly send for the watch, and deliver it without insisting upon any compensation, but on the contrary show him some gratitude, which in itself deserved five or ten pieces, he would send him to Newgate. The hapless watchmaker therefore had no alternative but to ask for the watch, and hand it back. The owner made a present to Hitchen of 3 gns for his trouble, while the watchmaker received no remuneration for his 50s.

Sometimes both men would be involved in certain individual cases, and their reluctance to co-operate resulted in some difficulties for the clients they were supposed to help. One such person was a biscuit-baker near Wapping who lost a pocketbook containing various papers, including an exchequer-bill for £100, and asked Wild to help him recover it. The latter advised him to advertise it and stop the payment of the bill, which he did accordingly. As the man heard nothing about it for a while, he came back several times to Wild, who at length told him that he had received a visit from a tall man with a long peruke and sword, calling himself the city-marshal, who asked him if he had lost his pocket-book. The biscuit-baker said he had, and wanted to know Hitchen's reasons for putting such a question, or whether he could give him any information. Hitchen replied he could tell him nothing as yet, but needed to know whether he had employed anybody to help search for it. The biscuit-baker answered that he had already used the services of Mr Wild.

This, Hitchen warned him, was a grave mistake, and he should have come straight to himself, the under-marshal, as the only person in England that could serve him. It was not within the power of Wild, or anyone else, to know where the pocketbook was. As he had it in his safe keeping, he asked what reward was to be offered. When the biscuit-baker said he would give £10, Hitchen said more would be necessary, as exchequer bills and similar items were ready money and could immediately be sold; and that, if he had employed him in the beginning and offered £40 or £50, he would have been glad to assist.

After the biscuit-baker had told Wild, the latter said he assumed the pocketbook was in the marshal's possession. There was no point in continuing to advertise it, as he was sure Hitchen would not have made any effort to find the biscuit-baker, unless he knew how to get at it. He advised the biscuit-baker to increase the reward, especially as the marshal had often told his servant how easily he could dispose of banknotes and exchequer-bills at gaming-houses, which he visited on a regular basis. The biscuit-baker returned to Hitchen, and bid £40 for his pocket-book and bill, but Hitchen told him he was too late as his exchequer bill had already ended up in the hands of others. Soon afterwards, some of the young pickpockets under Hitchen fell out in sharing the money that was given them for this pocketbook. One of them came to Wild, and discovered that he had sold the pocketbook, with the £100 exchequer-note in it, and other bills, to Hitchen, at a tavern in Aldersgate Street, for four or five guineas.

In another case, a man in a crowd at Charing Cross had his pocketbook stolen, containing bills and lottery-tickets worth several hundred pounds. At first it was publicly advertised with a £30 reward in the event of its safe return. Hitchen suspected that a famous pickpocket, well known for having a deformed hand, was responsible. He contacted the man, and in order to enforce a confession and delivery, told him confidently that he must be the person, as he had been described by the gentleman to have been near him, and whom he was certain had stolen his book. If the man brought him back the goods, he would be able to share in the reward; but if he refused to comply with such generous terms, he could not expect to come within the city gates again, or else he would end up in Bridewell or Newgate.

After several meetings, Hitchen's old friend admitted that he had the pocketbook, but told the marshal he did not expect such treatment from him, after the services he had done him, in concealing him several times, and thus keeping him out of gaol. This was not the way, he added, to expect any future service, when all his former good offices were forgotten. Yet Hitchen still insisted on his original terms. At length the pickpocket admitted defeat, considering that he could not repair to the Exchange, or elsewhere, to follow his pilfering employment, without the marshal's consent. Fearing revenge, he had had to part with the pocket-book upon terms reasonable between buyer and seller. Hitchen admitted that he had lost all his money the previous night at gaming, except a gold watch in his pocket. He was sure nobody would make any enquiries about it, as he had come into possession of it through an intrigue 'with a woman of the town', whom the gentleman would be ashamed to prosecute for fear of making his indiscretions public. Rather than risking the consequences of offending the all-powerful Hitchen, the pickpocket decided to let the matter rest.

One night, as they were near St Paul's, Hitchen and Wild met a crowd of pickpocket boys, who immediately ran away at the sight of their master. When Wild asked why, Hitchen told him they were a pack of rogues who were to have met him in the fields that morning, with a book he was informed they had taken from a gentleman, and they were afraid of being thrown into prison for their disobedience. One of them was the notorious young thief Jack Jones. 'We'll catch the whore's bird,' Hitchen vowed. Running behind a coach to make his escape, Jones was apprehended by both men. Hitchen took him to a tavern and threatened him severely, telling him he believed they were a bunch of housebreakers, and that they were involved in a burglary lately committed by four young criminals. As it happened he was correct, and the boy was so afraid that Hitchen had been informed, decided to confess for his own safety. Hitchen then promised to save his life if he was prepared to give evidence as a witness, then committed the boy to the Compter till the next morning, when he carried him before a Justice of the Peace, who took his information, and issued a warrant for the apprehension of his companions.

On learning that the gang would be found at a house in Beech Lane, Hitchen and Wild made a point of going there that same night. As they listened at the door, they overheard the boys and several others in mixed company. Entering the house, they met about a dozen people who angrily asked what business the marshal had there. They gave him a piece of their mind and he retreated, pulling the door after him, and leaving Wild to the mercy of the savage company.

Soon afterwards Hitchen returned with about ten watchmen and a constable, and asked the constable to go in at the door first, but the constable and marshal 'were both so long with their compliments' that the man thought neither of them would enter. At last the constable went in, with his long staff extended before him. Hitchen followed, asking what had happened to the villains, and why did the constable not secure them. Wild said they were under the table, and the constable pulled out the juvenile offenders, neither of whom were more than twelve years of age. They were committed to Newgate, but as the crime had taken place in the county of Surrey, they were afterwards removed to Marshalsea debtors' prison.

The next assizes were held at Kingston, and when Jones gave evidence against his companions before the grand jury, Hitchen supported him in giving evidence against the housebreakers. At the trial, the parents of the offenders appeared, and satisfied the Court that Hitchen's malign influence was totally responsible for the ruin of these boys, by taking them into the fields, and encouraging them to go stealing pocket-books. The judge noticed that the marshal seemed more intent in getting his hands on the reward than in seeing justice done, summed up the charge to the jury in favour of the boys, who were acquitted, and the marshal reprimanded. Hitchen was so angry at this, and so beside himself for not having accused them of other crimes, that he washed his hands of the business and immediately returned to London.

On the whole, Wild and Hitchen were successful in most of their joint encounters with the criminal underbelly of the City of London. Another evening they came across a clergyman standing against the wall in an alley, to which he had discreetly retired in order to answer the call of nature. Almost as soon as he had done so, a streetwalker looking for business brushed by, and the clergyman rather unwisely asked loudly what the woman wanted. Hitchen instantly rushed in upon them, and seized the clergyman, asking Wild to secure the woman. The clergyman resisted, protesting his innocence. Finding this to no avail, at length he asked to be allowed to go into an ironmonger's house nearby. Hitchen would not allow him to, and dragged him to the end of Salisbury Court, in Fleet Street, where he soon gathered a mob around him.

Two or three gentlemen who knew the parson happened to pass by at just that moment. They told the mob that they were dealing with the chaplain to a noble lord and asked what they were doing with him. The rough gentry answered that they thought he must have been the chaplain to the devil, as they had just caught him in the company of a whore. At this the gentlemen asked Hitchen if he would go with them to a tavern, so they could talk with him undisturbed, and he agreed. When they had reached the inn, the clergyman asked the marshal by what authority he thus abused him. Pulling out his staff, Hitchen replied he was a city officer, and would have him to the Compter, unless he gave very good security for his appearance next morning, when he would swear that he caught him with a fallen woman. Fearing exposure and embarrassment, the clergyman sent for other persons to vindicate his reputation, and they settled the matter by putting a purse of gold into the marshal's hand. Only then was the man of the cloth allowed to go on his way.

Hitchen was quite shameless in turning such situations to his own advantage, and exploiting the hospitality of his victims. On another night he was walking up Ludgate Hill when he noticed a well-dressed lady just in front of him. He told Wild that she must be a disreputable woman, as he had seen her talking with a man. Seizing her, he asked who she was, and she told him she was a bailiff's wife. This did not satisfy him, and he told her sharply that as she was more likely to be a whore, she would be taken to the Compter. When he seized her by the arm and took her through St Paul's Churchyard, she asked him if she could go and see her friends, but he would not let her. Instead he forced her into the Nag's Head, Cheapside, where he ordered a hot supper and plenty of wine, commanding her to keep at a distance from him, and telling her that he did not permit such vermin to sit in his company, though he intended to make her pay the reckoning.

When the supper was brought to the table he made short work of it, and would not allow her to eat with him, or to come near the fire, though it was a very cold night. After he had finished eating he looked around, and told her that if he had been an informer, or such a fellow, she would have called for food and wine herself, and not have given him the trouble of direction, or else she would have slipped a piece into his hand. She might do what she pleased, he added, but he assured her that it was in his power, if he saw a woman in the hands of informers, to discharge her and commit them. She replied that she had enough money herself to pay for the supper, at which he ordered his attendant to withdraw, while he compounded the matter with her.

When Wild returned, the gentlewoman was politely asked to sit by the fire, and eat the remainder of the supper. In all respects she was treated very kindly, only with a pretended reprimand that she should give him better language whenever he should speak to her for the future. After he had drunk another bottle of wine at her expense, she was discharged.

Before he had been suspended, Hitchen had daily meetings with the pickpocket boys in Moorfields, and treated them generously with cakes and ale, thus offering them a suitable incentive to continue their thefts on his behalf. At one stage one of the boys, more cunning than his companions, stole an alderman's pocket-book, and finding several bank bills inside, told Hitchen it was worth much more than the usual price. As the notes were of considerable value, he insisted on being given five guineas. Hitchen told the boy that such an amount would 'be enough to break him at once'. Two guineas would be quite sufficient, but if he had the good fortune to obtain a handsome reward, he would then make it up to five. This was enough to persuade the boy to deliver up the pocketbook. A few days afterwards, hearing that a very large reward had been given for the notes, he applied to Hitchen for the remaining three guineas as he had been promised. His 'reward' was to be told that he would be sent to the house of correction if he continued to demand it, and a peremptory reminder that such rascals as he were ignorant how to dispose of their money.

If Hitchen had any virtues, generosity was not one of them. Among the lessons Wild was learning was that it did not pay to be so mean and demanding in all his transactions, and that there would be times when some generosity of spirit was called for.

CHAPTER THREE

Wild the Thief-taker

Once he was fully reinstated in office in 1714, Hitchen found Wild was no longer merely a useful assistant. So faithfully had he learned the right lessons about their dubious craft that he had progressed to becoming a rival, and a dangerously successful one at that. The two masterminds had become bitterly jealous of each other, and could no longer work together. When they fell out, one of Wild's first manoeuvres of gang warfare was to eliminate as many of the thieves in Hitchen's control as he could. Unlike Hitchen, Wild did not merely receive goods or extort, but he also made money by informing on thieves (not usually his own) and apprehending them. His more ambitious and lucrative system of thief-taking combined the return of stolen goods with the prosecution of street robbers and other offenders whose conviction brought handsome rewards.

Now no longer answerable to anybody else, he began to pursue his own highly lucrative career as a thief-taker and receiver. By the end of 1714 he had moved from his house in Cock Alley to another in the Old Bailey, where despite all efforts by Hitchen to suppress his proceedings, his house became 'an Office of Intelligence for lost Goods'. Here he soon came to know all the thieves of note, from highwaymen and whores to thieves and forgers. In getting to know their methods, tricks and haunts, he gleaned a considerable amount of knowledge, and from becoming a mere confidant he became something of a director and mastermind.

His next stage was to open an 'Office of Intelligence for Lost Goods'. People who had been burgled were invited to call on him, and on arrival they were required to deposit a fee of one crown for his advice. He then asked their names, where they lived, where and how they were robbed, any details of time, place and manner that the goods became missing, if they suspected any persons and if so what kind of persons they were, the goods lost, and what reward was offered if they were returned. All this information was entered in a ledger. The persons were then assured that a careful inquiry would be made, and if they called again in two or three days he might be in a position to give them some news as to progress on finding them. This was done mainly to humour the enquirer, as Wild almost certainly knew all or nearly all there was to know about the circumstances of the robbery if not more.

When his client came back and wanted to know more, he said he had heard something of the goods, but the person he sent to enquire told him that the rogues had rejected his offer and pretended they could pawn them for more than the reward offered. If they were to be in a position to restore the goods to the rightful owner, it would have to be on better terms. However, if he could arrange a meeting with these rascals and speak to them, he was sure he could bring them to reason. He had little doubt that he could reach a satisfactory settlement, while at the same time suggesting that it would be just as well if his enquirer could slightly increase the reward offered. This enabled him to find out the largest sum likely to be given for the recovery of any property, and armed with this information, he asked the owner to apply at a particular time. By then the goods would probably be ready for delivery.

After one or two further meetings, Wild assured him that provided no questions were asked and so much money was given to the porter who brought them, the loser would have his things returned at such an hour precisely. This was done with all outward appearances of friendship, honest intention and generosity. When the client came to the last question, namely what Mr Wild expected for his trouble, a certain frostiness was noticeable on the thief-taker's part, as he answered with an air of equal pride and indifference that everything he ever did was purely from a principle of doing good to his fellow men. As to any matter of gratuity for the trouble he had taken, he left it totally to the enquirer that he might do what he thought fit. Even when money was presented to him he received it with 'the same negligent grace', always making the person feel that it was entirely his own choice, that he did it merely out of generosity, and that it was in no way the result of his request, that he took it as a favour, not as a reward.

The owners were so glad to regain their property without the trouble and expense of resorting to prosecution, that they regarded Wild as a friend and public benefactor. Sometimes they would give him up to half the value of the goods restored. A few more perspicacious individuals suspected he was not the knight in shining armour he pretended to be, and those who were dissatisfied with his superficial explanations might probe a little deeper, questioning him for further details as to how their goods had been discovered. When this happened he pretended that his feelings had been hurt at his honour being disputed thus, alleging that his only motive was to afford all the service in his power to the injured party, whose goods he imagined might possibly be those stopped by his friend. Since his honest intentions had been received so ungraciously, and since he himself was being interrogated respecting the robbers, he had nothing further to say on the subject, other than that his name was Jonathan Wild, and that if he could be of further assistance he was always available at his house in Cock Alley, Cripplegate. This generally had the required effect of making the interrogator feel guilty, and left him or them all the more ready to accede to what appeared his very reasonable demands.

Wild received in his own name no gratuity from the owners of these stolen goods, but always deducted his profit from the money which was to be paid to the broker. This enabled him to secure a considerable financial advantage without danger of prosecution, and for several years he managed to keep on the right side of the law.

He also had another clever scheme for profiting by the misfortunes of others. As soon as any major robbery was committed and reported, he already had some idea of who was responsible, and went to seek out the thieves. Rather than offering to buy the plunder in whole or in part, he made enquiries as to how the robbery was committed, where the victims lived, and what was taken away. He pretended to chide them for their behaviour, and telling them they should be more honest in future. Next he advised them to lodge everything they had taken in a proper place which he could recommend, and then promised he would personally take some measures for their security by getting the owners of the property some reward in return for restoring them again. Having thus wheedled the robbers into compliance with his measures, he divided the goods into different amounts and sent them to different places of safe keeping, while taking care to avoid having them in his own possession.

Next he went to contact those who had been robbed, and after offering his condolences, told them he had 'an acquaintance' with a broker to whom certain goods were brought, some of which he suspected had been stolen. Hearing that the person to whom he applied had been robbed, he said he thought it the duty of one honest body to another to inform them thereof, and to enquire what goods they had lost, in order to discover whether those they spoke of were the same or not.

People who suffered such losses were always ready to seize any opportunity of recovering their goods. Wild found it easy enough to make people listen to his terms. In a day or two they were sure to come again with intelligence that having called upon their friend and looked over the goods, they had found part of the goods there; and provided nobody was brought into trouble, and the broker had something in consideration of his care, they might be had again. He generally told the people, when they came on this errand, that he had heard of another parcel at such a place, and that if they waited a while, he would go and check whether they were one and the same.

By such means he perfected a cunning method of illegally amassing riches while appearing to be on the side of the law by running a gang of thieves, keeping the stolen goods, and waiting for the crime and theft to be announced in the newspapers. At this stage he would then claim that his 'thief taking agents', or police, had 'found' the stolen merchandise, and he would return it to its rightful owners for a small reward to meet the expenses of running his agents. Sometimes if the stolen items or circumstances allowed for blackmail, he did not wait for the theft to be announced. As well as 'recovering' these stolen goods, he would offer the constables aid in finding the thieves. These felons that Wild would help to 'discover' were in fact rivals or members of his own gang who had refused to cooperate with his taking the majority of the money, and he therefore had a vested interest in seeing them brought to justice.

He managed to find a loophole in an Act of 1706 which made receiving stolen property a felony, and acted as a kind of middleman who helped the victims of theft recover their goods, without ever keeping them in his possession. The papers now ran advertisements requesting 'all Sorts of strayed Valuables to be brought in to Mr. Wild's in the Old Bailey, upon Promise of great Rewards and no 'Questions' '. To the public he appeared to be performing a vital service, especially as he was cautious enough to refuse any fees, merely taking a large cut from the thieves. To preserve his reputation for honesty he would take measures to have these felons, or at any rate those whom he could not 'bring to comply' with him, apprehended and prosecuted. In doing so he was playing a skilful double game in which he acted the part of receiver and thief-taker who earned not only credit for bringing 'offenders to justice', but also the generous rewards offered by Parliament for the successful conviction of burglars and highwaymen.

His ability to hold his gang together, and the majority of his schemes, relied upon the widespread fear of theft and the nation's reaction to such wrongdoing. It was a crime to sell stolen goods, and low-level thieves ran a great risk in fencing their goods. He played on this by having his gang steal, either through pickpocketing or mugging, and then by 'recovering' the goods. He never explicitly sold them back, nor ever pretended that they were not stolen, while claiming at all times that he found the goods by policing, and publicly proclaimed his hatred of thieves. That very penalty for selling stolen goods gave him effective control of his gang, for he could turn in any of his thieves to the authorities at any time. By giving the goods to him for a cut of the profits, Wild's thieves were selling stolen goods, and if they did not give him their take to him, he would simply apprehend them as thieves.

What Wild did generally was use his thieves and ruffians to 'apprehend' rival gangs. He was by no means the first thief-taker who was actually a thief himself. Hitchen had shown the way by using his position as Under-Marshal to practice extortion, by pressurising brothels and pickpockets to pay him off or give him the stolen goods since purchasing the position in 1712, and as he had seen, such extortion was already an established practice at that time. The thieves were pleased as it was easier to steal small goods of sentimental value for which a good reward would be offered, than have to try to steal more valuable property that could be heavily protected.

In time Wild expanded his empire, divided London into districts, and set up gangs in each district, screening them from justice. He arranged for 'specialist' conmen and gangs that robbed churches, followed country fairs, ruled the prostitutes, or collected protection money. Though he did not lead any gangs he shamelessly organised and advised them, and passed on information about wealthy travellers to highwaymen. Any of his men who did not do his bidding, or crossed him, risked being reported to the authorities, and were very likely to find themselves being framed with the assistance of witnesses who were in his employ. Once they had been convicted, they could not testify against him in any subsequent court case, and the same happened to those who operated outside of his empire.

The rewards he gained from bringing criminals to justice helped him to rise in power among the criminal underworld. Favours done for him were never forgotten, and his loyalty to those who earned his respect never wavered. Nor did he ever forget the smallest act of treachery, and he was merciless in seeking revenge. He also turned in some of those depending on him to protect them from the law when he became tired of them, sometimes arresting them himself. At the same time he often joined the crowds at Tyburn when one of 'his' criminals was being executed, and he enjoyed passing on the tales of the men and women who were there due to his relentless pursuit of the criminal classes.

While careful to avoid handling stolen goods himself, he had artists and craftsmen to alter and reset jewellery and objects of art, and owned warehouses to store large amounts of goods. Later he kept a sloop for carrying stolen items to Holland, smuggling brandy, linen and lace to London on its return. His house was staffed by felons who had illegally returned from transportation. Knowing that they would be turned in if they displeased him gave them every incentive to serve him to the best of their abilities.

Thanks to Wild, articles which had previously been considered of little use but to the owners now became matters claiming particular attention from the thieves, by whom the metropolis and its environs were haunted. Pocket-books, which generally contained curious personal and therefore private memoranda, books of accounts, and other writings, being of great importance to the owners, produced particularly generous rewards. Banknotes, watches, rings, trinkets, and other articles of but small intrinsic worth, and other articles on which money could be readily procured, were now viewed as very profitable plunder. He was soon making such a good living by profiting from thefts of these that he could soon consider himself 'a man of consequence, took to dressing smartly in laced clothes, and wore a sword.

When he was released from the Compter Mary Milliner was his mistress, but around 1714 it was all over between them. There are different accounts as to why they went their separate ways. One suggested that they parted because she had such a bad reputation that he believed it would have harmed his cause to be seen as a bully who was merely in the service of someone with such a bad reputation as hers. They therefore parted amicably, and he found her network of criminal knowledge too valuable not to need to make use of it again in future. According to another account she was unwise enough to provoke him on some trivial matter, whereupon he struck her with his sword and cut off one of her ears. Yet another suggests that he cut off the ear simply to mark her out as a whore. Maybe he was restless by nature and soon grew tired of her, but it was said that in acknowledgment of the great services she had rendered him, by introducing him to so advantageous a profession, he granted her a weekly allowance until she died.

Throughout his life Wild had six 'wives' altogether. A liaison with Judith Nun about 1714/15 produced a daughter. Another short-term relationship soon afterwards was with Sarah Perrin, alias Gregstone or Grigson. Both women and the child survived him, but this second union produced no children, probably because he had become sterile through mercury treatment for syphilis. He then had a relationship with Elizabeth Mann, whom he treated as his common law wife and lived publicly with for about four or five years (which was not the case with either Nun or Perrin), until her death in late 1718 or early 1719. She was buried in St Pancras churchyard. In February 1719 he was believed to have married Mary Dean (née Brown), widow of John 'Skull' Dean, executed for burglary in 1717, at St Pancras Church, and she was thought to have died in or before 1732. The wedding was apparently well attended, but no record of the ceremony exists, probably as Wild destroyed it to avoid being charged with bigamy.

Now that he had such tight control over stolen goods and the activities of the thieves' network, he began to contact those who had been robbed, pretending to be greatly concerned at their misfortunes. It was their good fortune, he told them, that he had discovered some suspected property had been fallen into the hands of a very honest man, a broker, of his acquaintance. If their goods happened to be in the hands of his friend, they would be restored to the rightful owner. Needless to say, he also suggested that the broker should be rewarded for his trouble and disinterestedness, and he insisted on a promise that no disagreeable consequences should ensue to his friend, who had imprudently neglected to apprehend the supposed thieves.

At first glance this seemed to be an honest and good-natured act to persuade the thieves to restore the goods which they had stolen, and it was of some benefit to those who were robbed thus to have their goods again upon a reasonable premium. They would see that Wild or his mistress apparently took nothing, their advantages arising from what they took out of the gratuity left with the broker, and out of what they had bargained with the thief to be allowed of the money which they had procured him. To those who found such an advantage in it, the rewards were almost equivalent to the price now given by receivers, since receiving was now too dangerous, and they also reaped a certain security by the bargain.

Two factors contributed to his survival in such a risky enterprise. One was the readiness the government always showed in detecting persons guilty of capital offences, in which instances they not only pardoned the guilty but also offered rewards, as long as they made some discovery which led to the apprehension of the more serious felons. Wild used this privileged position with a kind of authority, taking upon himself the mantle of an unofficial Minister of Justice. However ill-founded, this assumed appearance proved of great advantage to him. The other point which contributed to keep him from any prosecutions on the score of these illegal and unwarrantable actions was the great willingness of people who had been robbed to recover their goods, and who, provided they could regain their valuable possessions for a small consideration, were so far from making an effort to bring the offenders to justice that they thought the premium a cheap price to get off.

Wild was never an operator, or a practicer in any one branch of thieving. In effect, he had made himself a kind of Director General of the united forces of highwaymen,

The Tyburn Tree, *from an eighteenth-century engraving*

housebreakers, footpads, pickpockets, and private thieves. During his years of success, it was the easiest of easy money. He continually encouraged the thieves in his gangs to let him know punctually what goods they had stolen at any time, so he could always or nearly always give a direct answer to those who came to make enquiries after they had been robbed, either by their own carelessness, or by the dexterity of the thief. To those who complied faithfully with his instructions, he was a certain protector on all occasions, even to the extent of helping to procure them liberty when apprehended, either in committing a robbery, or upon the information of one of the gang.

Should his thieves threaten to display any sign of independence, and defy his rules, try for the sake of a quick profit to sell the goods they stole without keeping him informed, make any threats against their companions, or grumble at the orders he gave them, he took the first opportunity of telling them that he was well assured they 'did ill and plundered poor honest people, to indulge themselves in their debaucheries; that they would do well to think of amending before the Justice of their country fell upon them'. After such a warning they could not expect any further help from him, if they were to fall foul of the law. If any further admonition was necessary, they would be apprehended, find themselves in Newgate and then before the court, and unless they were extremely fortunate, end up on the gallows at Tyburn. Wild could thus be sure of procuring any rewards offered, of demonstrating to the relieved owners his ability to restore their goods to them, and also of showing his effectiveness in catching and punishing the guilty.

It was said that during his fifteen years or so as a thief-taker, he brought more villains to the gallows than any other man ever did. By keeping their numbers down, he made London a little more safe for law-abiding persons to travel or even to reside with security in their own houses. Against that verdict, it should be admitted that the City would have been safer still had it not been for his own criminal masterminding activities.

His credit soared in the spring of 1716, when he brought to justice several street robbers who had killed a lady during a vicious assault and robbery. At around the same time he inserted an advertisement in the London Gazette, describing himself as a man whose business it was to apprehend thieves, and bring them to Justice, thus furthering the impression that he was acting in a semi-official capacity. By January 1717 he was openly proclaiming himself to be the 'Head Thief Catcher', or 'Thief-catcher General of Great Britain'.

All this seemed a remarkably clever way of staying just on the right side of the law, ensuring that no blame could be laid at his door. He could disclaim any involvement in the robbery, for he neither saw the thief who took away the goods, nor received them after they were taken. The method he pursued in order to procure the things again was neither dishonest or illegal. His position was merely one of enquiring among such people of dubious reputation as he acknowledged he knew. Whenever he heard that such a robbery was committed at such a time, and any particular goods were taken, he took steps to let the thief be well aware that if he had any regard for his own safety, he would ensure that the stolen goods were taken to a specific place, and as a result he might reasonably hope for some reward. If the thief returned the items, no guilt or blame could be laid upon Wild himself. If the items were not returned, then the thief could be reasonably sure that his days were numbered.

There were considerable advantages to be derived by Wild from examining the people who had been robbed in this way. It helped him to find out details of any goods which the thieves might omit to mention, and thus gave him information should they decide not to 'declare' any of their ill-gotten gains. Being in possession of the secrets of every notorious thief, they had little choice but to comply with whatever terms Wild intended to impose on them. Any opposition on their part would render them liable to being turned over by him to the authorities.

When the rogues with whom Wild was in league faithfully gave him details of the robberies they had committed, and entrusted him with the disposal of their booties, he assured them that they might safely rely on him for protection against the vengeance of the law. His artful behaviour, and the punctuality with which he discharged his engagements, brought him complete confidence among all his thieves. If he made them aware that he wanted to see them, and that he would not deliver them to the authorities, they would attend him without hesitation, without entertaining any apprehension of danger, although they were conscious that he had information against them, and that their lives were absolutely in his power. If they rejected his proposals, or failed to co-operate in any other way, he would warn them that he had given them his word that they could come and go in safety, but they would do well to take care of themselves thereafter. Should they ever see him again, they would find in him a bitter foe.

This great influence that Wild obtained over the thieves was hardly surprising. When he promised every effort to rescue them from impending fate, he was usually successful. He would never interfere with those who towed the line, but gave them every encouragement for going about their thieving ways. Should they be apprehended by anyone else, he nearly always managed to secure their discharge and set them free.

His most usual method in desperate cases, and when matters could not be managed with more ease and expedition, was to assure any third party that they would willingly give evidence, under the pretext that it was in their power to make discoveries of great importance to the common good. When they were in prison he frequently attended them, and supplied them with any particulars which he thought it would be prudent for them to relate to the Court. When his accomplices were apprehended, and he could not prevent their being brought to trial, he managed by various means to keep the principal witnesses out of Court, and the delinquents were generally dismissed for sheer lack of evidence by which they might be convicted.

Wild always looked after his own, but was an implacable enemy to those strong or foolish enough to reject his terms, and to take it into their heads to dispose of their stolen effects for their own separate advantage. In these cases he spared no effort to surrender them into the hands of justice, and as he always knew where they would be found, for them there was no hiding place. By his subjecting those who incurred his displeasure to the punishment of the law, he always managed to obtain the rewards offered for pursuing them to conviction; greatly extended his ascendancy over the other thieves, who considered him with a kind of awe, and at the same time established his character as being a man of great public utility.

It was his normal practice to give instructions to the thieves whom he employed as to the manner in which they should conduct themselves, and if they followed his directions they were usually successful. Those who failed to observe his rules strictly enough, or who were guilty of any kind of mismanagement or error in the prosecution of the schemes he had suggested, could expect to be convicted at the next sessions, as he considered them inept or unsuited for what was regarded as 'the profession of roguery'.

Sometimes he was asked how he could possibly carry on the business of restoring stolen effects, and yet not be in league with the robbers. To this he always answered blandly that his acquaintance among thieves was very extensive. Whenever he received information about a robbery, he made enquiries after the suspected parties, and left word at the right places that, if the goods were left where he recommended, the reward would be paid with no questions asked. 'Surely no imputation of guilt can fall upon me,' he concluded, 'for I hold no interviews with the robbers, nor are the goods given into my possession.'

Among his clients who had reason to be grateful for his services at around this time were the servants of a lady of fortune who was visiting Piccadilly. They left her sedan at the door, and went to refresh themselves at a neighbouring public house. When they returned there was no sign of the vehicle, so they went to Wild at his office, reported it, handed over the usual fee, and were asked to call back upon him in a few days. When they kept the appointment he extorted from them a considerable reward, and then told them to attend the chapel in Lincoln's Inn Fields on the following morning, during the time of prayers. A little puzzled, they did as they were told, and when they arrived at the place of worship, under the piazzas of the chapel they saw the chair, examined it and found that not only had it suffered no damage, but still contained the velvet seat, curtains, and all other furniture as before.

Lincoln's Inn Fields, showing the hall, chapel and Chancery Court

A more serious episode occurred on 31 March 1716 when a young man, John Knap, accompanied his mother to Sadler's Wells. On their way home at about ten in the evening they were attacked near the wall of Gray's Inn Gardens by five villains. Knap was knocked down, and his alarmed mother called at once for help. One of the men fired his pistol at her, and she was killed instantly. A large reward was offered by proclamation in the London Gazette for the discovery and bringing to justice of the person or persons responsible; and Wild was remarkably assiduous in his efforts to apprehend them. From a description given of some of the villains, he immediately had a good idea of who the gang members were, namely William White, Thomas Thurland, John Chapman alias Edward Darvel, Timothy Dun, and Isaac Rag. Exactly eight days later, on the evening of Sunday, 8 April, he learned that some of them were drinking with a group of prostitutes at a house kept by John Weatherly, in Newtoner's Lane. He went to Weatherly's, accompanied by his assistant Abraham, who played a similar role to that which he had had under Hitchen, and seized White, whom he brought away about midnight in a hackney-coach, and lodged him in the roundhouse.

Not long afterwards he was told that a certain James Aires was at the Bell Inn, Smithfield, in company with a woman of the town. Accompanied by his assistants, Wild went to the inn, and under the gateway they met Thurland, who had been mistaken for Aires. Thurland had two brace of pistols, but after he was suddenly seized, he was deprived of any opportunity of making use of them, and was taken into custody. On the following night they went to a house in White Horse Alley, Drury Lane, where they apprehended Chapman. Soon after the murder of Mrs Knap, Chapman and others stopped the coach of Thomas Middlethwaite, who protected himself from robbery by discharging a blunderbuss, and wounding Chapman in the arm. At this point the other villains discreetly retired.

A little while later, Wild received information charging Isaac Rag with a burglary, and apprehended him at a public house in St Giles's which he used to frequent.

When he was taken in front of the magistrates, in the course of his examination Hag impeached twenty-two of his accomplices, charging them with being housebreakers, footpads, and receivers of stolen effects, and as a result was admitted an evidence for the crown. Rag had already been convicted of a misdemeanour in January 1714, and sentenced to stand three times in the pillory. He had concealed himself in a dust hole at the house of Thomas Powell, where he was discovered and searched. A pistol, some matches, and a number of pick-lock keys were found in his possession. He was evidently intending to commit a burglary, but as he never entered the house, he was indicted for a misdemeanour in entering the yard with intent to steal. In October 1715 he was indicted for burglary in Elizabeth Stanwell's house the previous August, but acquitted of the charge.

White, Thurland, and Chapman were arraigned on 18 May 1716 at the Old Bailey, on an indictment for assaulting John Knap, 'putting him in fear', and stealing from him a hat and wig on 31 March. They were also indicted for the murder of his mother Mary Knap, widow, on the same date, whom White had shot dead. At the same time they were indicted on a separate charge of assaulting and robbing John Gough. White was a fourth time indicted with James Russell for a burglary in the house of George Barclay, and Chapman was a fourth time indicted for a burglary in the house of Henry Cross. All three were sentenced to death and executed at Tyburn on 8 June.

Wild spared little effort in apprehending Timothy Dun, who had previously escaped the long arm of the law by going to a new lodging and concealing himself. Though Dun had managed to escape for a while, Wild was confident of discovering him again, as he knew he would not be able to hide from him for long and was bound to return to his old ways. He was so sure of success that he made a wager of ten guineas that he would have Dun in custody by a certain time. The latter soon lost patience with having to remain in hiding, and sent his wife to go and ask Wild whether he was still in danger of being apprehended. He told her he could not give her an answer, and when she left, Wild ordered one of his people to follow her home. She took a glass of water at Blackfriars, and then stopped at the Falcon Inn. Suspecting that the man lurking nearby had been sent to trace her, she stopped for another glass of water, and crossed to Whitefriars. Noticing she was still being followed, she ordered the waterman to try and give him the slip by proceeding to Lambeth. By the time she had landed there, it was almost dark. She assumed that she must have escaped the observation of Wild's man by now, and immediately walked home. However he was still on her trail and traced her to Maid Lane, near the Bankside, Southwark. When he saw her enter a house, he marked the wall with chalk, and then returned to Wild to tell him.

On the next morning Wild and his assistant Abraham, one of his associates, Mr Riddlesden, and another man, went to the house where the woman had been seen to enter. Dun heard a noise, and suspecting that he had been discovered, got through a back-window on the second floor on the roof of the pantry, the bottom being about eight feet from the ground. Abraham discharged a pistol, and wounded Dun in the arm. He fell from the pantry into the yard, then Riddlesden also fired, and wounded him in the face. Dun was secured and taken to Newgate, tried at the next sessions, and executed at Tyburn.

Riddlesden had originally studied law as a career, but soon drifted into bad ways. His life of crime began when he broke into the chapel at Whitehall, and stole the communion-plate. He was caught, convicted and sentenced to death, but this was commuted to transportation for seven years. On his release he went to America for a while, but returned to England as soon as he could, and had an affair a young lady, daughter of a wealthy merchant from Newcastle-upon-Tyne. Before he could get his hands on her considerable fortune, he was apprehended for some unrecorded offence and imprisoned in Newgate. By now she was pregnant with his child, went into the prison to be with him and had her confinement there, but her friends traced her and fetched her back home. Next, after his association with Wild, he had a relationship with the widow of Richard Revel, one of the Newgate turnkeys. She went with him to Philadelphia as his wife, though whether they were ever legally married or not is unrecorded, but after a disagreement between them she returned to England, and took a public house in Golden Lane. What became of Riddlesden is unknown.

There were inevitably limits to Wild's ability to manipulate the system, as was demonstrated by the case of Arnold Powell, a notorious thief. Powell was arrested after having robbed a house in the neighbourhood of Golden Square of a large amount of property, and was sent to Newgate. Wild came to visit him, telling him that he was prepared to save his life for a certain sum. If his proposal was rejected, Powell would almost certainly be hanged at Tyburn for his crime. The prisoner did not believe that Wild could cause him any harm, but neither did he trust his offer of help, and declined his services. In due course he was brought to trial, but acquitted through a defect of evidence for the prosecution. Wild then found out that Powell had been responsible for another burglary, in the house of a Mr Eastlick, near Fleet Ditch, and he proposed that the latter should bring Powell to justice for the offence. When informed that he was to be charged, Powell realised that he would need Wild's services after all. He sent for him, and a compromise was reached according to the terms which Wild himself had proposed, in consequence of which Powell was assured that his life should be spared.

Shortly before the sessions were due, Wild informed the prosecutor that the first and second days would be taken up with other trials, and as he was willing Mr Eastlick should avoid attending with his witnesses longer than was necessary. Timely notice was to be given when Powell would be arraigned. But Eastlick arranged to have the prisoner put to the bar, and as nobody came to give any counsel for the prosecution Powell was ordered to be taken away. After some time he was again brought before the bar, then ordered away, and afterwards put up a third time. On each occasion, proclamation was made for the prosecutor to appear. At length the jury were charged with the prisoners and, as no accusation was brought against him, he was dismissed and the Court ordered an adjournment.

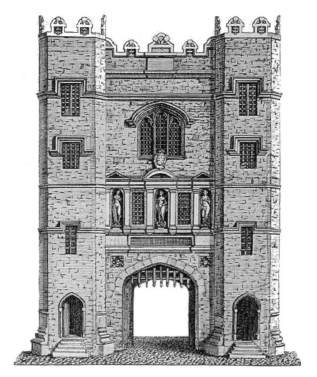

Newgate Prison, the gateway

Nevertheless Powell was ordered to remain in custody till the next sessions, as there was yet another indictment against him. Eastlick, a law-abiding citizen who was aware of Wild's offer to try and help Powell regain his liberty for a fee, informed the Court. Wild was reprimanded with some severity. Powell tried to feign illness in order to avoid being brought to trial the next sessions, but it was to no avail. He was arraigned, convicted and executed on 20 March 1716.

Within a few years Wild had sharply reduced Hitchen's own tame group of thieves. A bitterly jealous Hitchen was foolish enough to let himself be provoked into making their rivalry common knowledge in 1718 when he attempted to expose Wild with *A True Discovery of the Conduct of Receivers and Thief-Takers in and about the City of London*. This diatribe called Wild the chief manager and source or 'The Regulator' of crime, accusing him of manipulating evidence to convict and hang minor offenders while protecting greater villains and profiting from the return of stolen valuables. He was not a 'Thief-Taker' as he claimed, more a 'Thief-Maker', who perverted the good intentions of law and order by manipulating and stifling the testimony of witnesses to protect his own on one hand, and hang those criminals who were no longer of use to him, or defying his authority, on the other.

Secure in the knowledge that the public and authorities were on his side, Wild retorted with An Answer to a Late Insolent Libel. In this he explained that Hitchen, his former 'Grand Master in Iniquity', had employed him as an assistant to run thieves, an activity which he had nothing to do with, and that Hitchen profited from the thefts carried out by numerous young pickpockets in the City. It also revealed the previously well-kept secret of Hitchen's homosexuality by telling how the marshal had taken him to a molly-house, one of several clubs for homosexuals established in London in the early decades of the eighteenth century.

Hitchen tried to turn these charges aside by reissuing his condemnation of Wild in a slightly enlarged version, under a new title, *The Regulator, or, A Discovery of the Thieves, Thief-Takers and Locks*. However it was too late for Hitchen to restore his reputation which was now tarnished beyond repair, his credibility in tatters. A series of exchanges in the press ended with one editor adamantly refusing to be bullied any more by 'Tom Teltruth', or Hitchen, who had shown that his word could no longer be relied on. His prior suspensions from duties and the shocking charge of homosexuality eliminated him as a threat to Wild. However he continued his position as Under City Marshal and presumably continued to profit corruptly from his office, though on a lesser scale as fewer people now trusted him. The Under City Marshal had challenged his former pupil turned feared rival – and lost.

CHAPTER FOUR

Wild and the 1718 Transportation Act

It was perhaps only to be expected that Wild's highly profitable career would not continue unchecked for long. At first he had found it easy to dispose of stolen goods for a reasonable value. However thieving was becoming such a serious problem that Parliament was eventually compelled to act, in order to provide for the punishment of receiving stolen goods. In 1718 a Transportation Act was passed, containing a clause which made it a capital offence to accept any reward in consequence of restoring stolen effects, and made it a felony to receive stolen goods, knowing them to be stolen, without attempting to prosecute the thief. Anyone convicted of receiving goods, knowing them to have been the proceeds of robbery, was liable to a sentence of fourteen years' transportation. The clause read:

> And whereas there are several persons who have secret acquaintance with felons, and who make it their business to help persons to their stolen goods, and by that means gain money from them, which is divided between them and the felons, whereby they greatly encourage such offenders: Be it enacted by the authority aforesaid, that wherever any person taketh money or reward, directly or indirectly, under pretence or upon account of helping any person or persons to any stolen goods or chattels, every such person so taking money or rewards as aforesaid (unless such person do apprehend, or cause to be apprehended, such felon who stole the same, and cause such felon to be brought to his trial for the same, and give evidence against him) shall be guilty of felony, and suffer the pains and penalties of felony, according to the nature of the felony committed in stealing such goods and chattels, in the manner and with such circumstances as the same were stolen.

The principal architect of this legislation was William Thomson, Solicitor-General for England and Wales. Its main aim was to act as a curb on Wild's practices, and it was sometimes known as the 'Jonathan Wild Act'. Rumour had it that Thomson unofficially took Wild gently to one side, warned him that his activities were considered suspect, and if he did not mend his ways, he stood in danger of committing a capital offence.

Even if he had not been given such advice, Wild was too intelligent not to realise that the Act was a serious threat to his way of life. He therefore closed his office, although he carried on his work in the coffeehouses and on the streets, and continued to place advertisements in newspapers offering rewards with no questions asked.

Yet he could not renounce his thief-taking ways completely. In order to try and circumvent the penalties now enshrined in the legislation, he summoned a meeting of all the thieves with whom he had connections, telling them that if they took their stolen goods to unscrupulous pawnbrokers, they could barely expect to receive a quarter of their value. If the goods were offered to strangers, the thieves would probably be turned over to the authorities. He was sure that the 'most industrious thieves' had great difficulty in earning a livelihood, and many had to reconcile themselves to an existence barely above starvation level, or being forever 'in great and continual danger of Tyburn'. However he had a plan for removing such inconveniences. They must follow his advice, and behave towards him with honour. In conclusion, he warned them firmly that when they made any finds, they should deliver them to him, not to the pawnbroker. He, Wild, would undertake to restore goods to the owners and raise a better sum this way, while the thieves themselves would remain safe from detection.

Naturally this proposal was favourably received. It would have been a brave thief, or a very foolish one, who dared to get on the wrong side of Wild. If all the stolen effects were handed over to him, he would appoint convenient places where they must be deposited, as it would never do for him to have them left at his own house. For a while he thought it would be safer to stop receiving money from persons who had been robbed and came to seek his advice. But the more persistent, those who came to call on him two or three times about their lost goods, would merely be informed that all he had been able to learn respecting their business was that if a sum of money was taken to a particular place, their property would be restored the same day, duly delivered to the person who handed the money over. Once this was agreed a porter was called, and directions given him to go and wait at the corner of the street. As he came to the place, or was on his way there, he was met by somebody who delivered him the goods upon his paying the money. At other times the owners of the goods, on their way home, were overtaken by a stranger who put the goods into their hands with a note, on which was written the amount they were required to pay for them.

Sometimes, as the person robbed was returning from Wild's house, he was accosted in the street by a man who delivered the stolen effects. This man would at the same time produce a note mentioning the sum that was to be paid for them. In cases where he considered there might be some danger, he advised people to advertise that whoever would bring the stolen goods to Jonathan Wild should be rewarded, and no questions asked.

As he was still careful to ensure that it could never be proved that he either saw the thief, received the goods, or accepted a reward, and acted agreeably to the directions of the injured party, there was no reason to identify him as being hand in glove with the felons. When those who had recovered their property asked him what they should give him for his trouble, he told them that what he had done was without any self-interest, and merely from a principle of doing good, so he would make no claim. If he accepted a present, he should not consider it as being his due, but as an instance of generosity, which he should acknowledge accordingly.

Those who had been robbed were as willing as ever to recover their goods with as little trouble as possible, and so they easily fell into Wild's measures. If the person was too inquisitive, as happened on occasion, he said he only came to serve them, and they were mistaken if they thought otherwise. He told them that if goods were offered to pawn by a suspected person, the broker had the honesty to stop them; 'and therefore, Sir, if you question me about thieves, I have nothing to say to you but that I can give a good account of myself'. This usually put an end to any argument, and those who sought his help would nearly always be prepared to deal with him on his own terms.

All this time, as Wild had his profits out of what was paid to the broker, he took no money from those to whom he restored the goods. This enabled him to protect the integrity of his good reputation, especially as there was no law in being that could affect him adversely. However he found it necessary to modify his practices. He no longer applied to those who had lost anything, but they had to apply to him if they expected his assistance.

Realising that he ran the risk of losing his good name, he was careful not to allow any discontent to appear among his followers. He found it would be as well to ensure that, whenever he promised them his protection, such an undertaking should not be neglected or pass unfulfilled. Where his influence among persons in authority was not enough to enable him to get his own way, his efforts in procuring the testimony of false witnesses to rebut any detailed evidence for the prosecution, and the nature of which he could always discover for himself beforehand, generally ensured him success. His threats to those who offended or crossed him were fulfilled as faithfully as his promises, and once he declared vengeance on anyone who had crossed him, such unlucky souls could be sure that he would be as good (or as bad) as his word. By his subjecting those who incurred his displeasure to the punishment of the law he obtained the rewards offered for pursuing them to conviction, and greatly extended his standing over the other thieves, who considered him their leader. At the same time, he was able to promote himself as a conscientious public servant who worked for the public good.

After 1718, perhaps to 'support his Credit with the Magistrates' and to divert attention away from his effective role as a receiver, perhaps simply because he had become arrogant with success, Wild focused more and more on the very public business of gang breaking and thief-taking. His reputation stood so high that the Privy Council consulted with him on ways of controlling crime, particularly the ways and means of checking the recent and rather alarming increase in highway robberies. Not surprisingly he recommended that the gratuities for those who gave evidence against thieves should be raised. In May 1720 a Royal Proclamation increased the reward for capturing a thief from £40 to £100, and within another few months to £140, for the successful conviction of robbers in the vicinity of London, or specifically within five miles of Charing Cross. He became a regular fixture at the Old Bailey and other criminal courts where he was called to give evidence for the prosecution, or 'scarce an Assize or Sessions past but Jonathan slew his Man'. Soon his divide and conquer tactics began to elicit complaints from defendants, one of whom in 1723 openly called Wild a villain who made his living by 'swearing away' the lives of honest men.

Around this time he was involved in at least one instance of theft by a child, although it proved impossible to prove that he was responsible. Whether it was sheer coincidence that he happened to know the guilty party, or whether he was actually training the lad in question to steal, is open to speculation, but the latter explanation was certainly possible. One day a boy aged about nine or ten came to the front door of a surgeon carrying some vials, or small glass medicine bottles, in a basket which he used to bring around and offer for sale. It was bitterly cold winter weather outside, and the boy complained he was almost frozen to death as well as starving. The surgeon's maid took pity on him, showed him into the kitchen, and gave him a bowl of milk and bread, with a lump or two of sugar. He ate a little, then said he had enough, thanked her, and marched off with a silver spoon, and a pair of forceps which had been lying around in the shop as he came in. Though everybody had seen the boy in the kitchen, nobody suspected him at first.

The surgeon knew Wild, who lived nearby, went to his office, paid the fee and was about to tell him how the items went missing, but Wild cut him short and sent him into the next room, and much to his surprise he immediately saw his forceps and silver spoon lying upon the table. He had hardly taken them up to look at them before Wild followed him, saying he assumed the man had no further need for his assistance. The surgeon said that there were a great many servants in his family, and some of them would certainly be blamed for the theft. Would Mr Wild kindly let him know how they were stolen?

The thief, Wild assured him, was not far away, and if the surgeon would give him his word that the culprit would come to no harm, he would produce him immediately. The gentleman readily agreed, Wild went out briefly, and brought the boy back with him, asking the surgeon if he knew him. The latter admitted he did, but had never imagined that such a small child could have had so much wickedness in him. However, as he had given his word, and as he had his items back, he would not only overlook the matter this time, but if the would bring his bottles again as usual, he would continue to make use of his custom. Less than a week later the boy came to offer his wares once more. The surgeon bought some as usual, then ordered his cook to warm some milk over the fire, added two ounces of sugar, crumbled it with a couple of penny loaves, and ordered the light-fingered young hawker to eat every drop - and then kindly but firmly escorted him out through the door before he had a chance to get up to further mischief.

Another case arose when a dealer in silks with premises near Covent Garden had a magnificent piece of rich damask, which he meant to use for the suit of a certain Duke for his birthday. The lace-man brought the trimming necessary, the mercer had made it up in a parcel, tied it at each end with blue ribbon, sealed it carefully, and placed it on one end of the counter, ready for his Grace's servant to call for it that afternoon. The man arrived, but when the mercer went to deliver him the goods, the piece could not be found. As the master had been all day in the shop, he could not blame any of his servants of dishonesty or carelessness. The only thing he could do was to go and see Wild which he did, told him the problem, offered the fee, and answered the usual questions. Soon he lost patience, and told Wild that the loss he had sustained, though the intrinsic value of the goods was very little, lay more in his disobliging his customer. If Mr Wild could tell him in a few words, if it was in his power, he had thirty guineas ready to pay him, but if he expected him to dance attendance for a week or two, he would not part with more than half the money. Feigning an air of injured innocence, Wild begged him to have a little more consideration. He was no thief, nor no receiver of stolen goods, but merely needed some time to enquire – or else the man might go away and take whatever measures he pleased.

As he saw that this would leave him without any hope of getting his precious material back, the mercer began to talk more mildly, and begged Wild to think of something to help him immediately. Wild went outside for a minute or two, and then returned to tell the gentleman that it was not in his power to serve him in such a hurry, if at all, but in a day or two he might be able to give him some answer. The mercer insisted that a day or two would lessen the value of the goods one half to him, and Wild insisted sharply that it was not in his power to do anything sooner. Then a servant came in a hurry, and told Wild a gentleman below needed to speak with him. Wild told the mercer he would come back to him in one minute. Without staying for a reply he went out, shutting the door firmly after him.

In about five minutes he returned smiling, as he told his client he was the luckiest man he ever knew. He had just spoken to one of his people, asked him to go to a house where he know some thieves used to gather, make enquiries about the robbery just committed in his house, and to say that the gentleman had been with him and offered thirty guineas, provided everything was returned. The man had declared that if they were not restored to him very soon, he would give as great a reward for the discovery of the thief or thieves, whom he would not hesitate to prosecute with the utmost severity. Wild assured him this would be unnecessary, and if the mercer would go home straightaway, he would hear more about it before long. He should remember that the thirty guineas reward had been his own offer and he was at liberty to offer it or change his mind, but Wild had done everything for him he possibly could, without any expectation of a gratuity.

The mercer left, very puzzled, wondering how the matter would be resolved. As he walked up Southampton Street another man overtook him, patted him on the shoulder, and delivered him the bundle of missing material unopened, telling him the price was twenty guineas. The mercer paid him at once, returned to Wild about half an hour later, thanked him profusely, and begged him to accept the ten guineas he had saved him for his trouble. Wild told him that he had saved him nothing, but supposed that the people thought the twenty guineas he had just paid would be enough, especially as those concerned were now safe from prosecution. The mercer insisted that Wild should accept the ten guineas. Wild took them from his hand and returned him five of them, assuring him that would more than suffice, as it was satisfaction enough to an honest man that he was able to help people get their goods again.

Also making use of his services at this time was a lady whose husband had gone overseas for a while and had sent her drafts worth between £1500 and £2000. She lost the pocket-book containing them, between Bucklersbury and Magpie alehouse in Leadenhall Street, where the merchant lived upon whom they had been drawn. When she asked him to help he advised her to go straight to Wild. She went to see him in his office, paid his fee and answered his question. He told her that perhaps in an hour or two, some of his people might hear who had picked her pocket. She was so anxious to have the pocket-book back that she offered a hundred guineas, to which he answered that though they were of much greater value to her, yet they could not be worth anything like it to them. She should therefore keep her own counsel, say nothing in the hearing of his people, and he would give her the best directions he could for the recovery of her notes. Meanwhile, if she would go to any tavern nearby, and try to eat some dinner, he would bring her an answer before the cloth was taken away. As she did not know any nearby taverns, he suggested the Baptist Head, but she was uncomfortable about going on her own and said she was not prepared to go there unless he promised to come and eat with her.

With some misgivings she made her way to the inn on her own, and ordered a plate of chicken and sausages. She waited three quarters of an hour, and when he eventually arrived he told her he had heard news of her book. Perhaps she would be so good as to place ten guineas upon the table, in case they should be needed. As the cook came up to say the food was ready, Jonathan asked her to go and see whether there was a woman waiting at his door. She went to look, and when she noticed a woman in a scarlet riding-hood walk by Wild's house, curiosity prompted her to go closer. Then she remembered she had left the guineas on the table upstairs, went and fetched them without a word to Wild, and then running down again went towards the woman in the red hood, who was still walking around outside.

At this stage the woman came up to her, handed her the pocket book, and asked her to open it and check everything was safe. The lady did so, and seeing everything was in order, the woman in the red riding-hood presented her with 'another little note' upon which she gave her a little billet, on the outside of which was written ten guineas. The lady delivered her the money immediately, told Wild how pleased she was to have her book back, and now she could eat her dinner. After their table had been cleared away, she said she thought it was time for her to go to the merchant. Believing it would be necessary to make Wild a present for his trouble, she put her hand in her pocket, and was most surprised to find her green purse gone, with the rest of the fifty guineas she had borrowed from the merchant that morning. Though she looked confused, she said nothing. Wild asked her what was the matter, and she said she was amazed that the woman took only ten guineas for the book, yet at the same time picked her pocket of thirty-nine. He begged her not to worry, assuring her she should not lose one farthing, then went back to his house.

Less than half an hour his assistant Abraham entered the room, told him the woman had been found, and was about to be taken to the Compter. Wild turned to the lady, telling her that she would see 'what exemplary punishment' he would give 'this infamous woman'. Then turning to Abraham, he asked if the green purse of money had been found on her. The agent confirmed that it was, and the lady said she would take the purse gladly but did not wish to prosecute the poor wretch for the world. Wild then whispered to Abraham, and sent him out. No sooner was the latter gone than Wild told the lady that she would be too late at the merchant's unless they took a coach, which they accordingly did, and stopped by the Compter gate by the Stocks Market. At first she was rather puzzled, but by the time they had been in a tavern a short while, back came Abraham with the green purse containing the gold. He said to Wild that the lady had only used a guinea of the money for food and wine, and all the rest was there. Wild told him to hand it back to her, and asked her to check it was all there. She counted it out carefully, and found there were forty-nine guineas. With astonishment, she said that the woman must be bewitched, as she had sent ten guineas more than she should have had.

Shaking his head, Wild told her that the woman had sent her back again the ten guineas which she received for the book. He personally did not hold with any such practices, and had ordered the thief to give up the money she had just taken in addition to what she had stolen. Therefore he hoped, whatever the lady might think of her, that she would not have a worse opinion of her humble servant for this accident. Thoroughly confused by now, the lady then said the very least she could do was to ask Wild to accept ten guineas as a gratuity. He declined, saying that he scorned all actions of such a sort as much as any man of quality in the kingdom. All the reward he wanted was that she would acknowledge he had acted honourably, then he got up, bowed and went downstairs.

Wild moved to Dulwich for a time, and opened another office in Newtoner's Lane. One of his next clients was a lady who had her pocket picked of £7,000 in banknotes. She gave Abraham details, and in a few days he apprehended a notorious gang of three pickpockets. When he took them to Wild, they handed the money back, and were dismissed. After Abraham had returned the money to the owner she made him a present of £400, which he gave to Wild. The pickpockets were later arrested for some other offences, and sentenced to transportation.

As Wild found it difficult to manage without having the faithful Abraham nearby, he only kept his Newtoner's Lane office for three months. About a week after he returned from Dulwich to the City of London, a mercer in Lombard Street ordered a porter to take a box containing goods valued at £200 to a particular inn. While on his way the porter was watched by three thieves. One of them was more smartly dressed than his companions, and he told the man that if he was willing to earn sixpence, he should go to the tavern at the end of the street, and ask for the cloak he had left at the bar. In case the waiter should prove reluctant to give it to him, he should take his gold watch as a token. The man went to the tavern, and, having delivered his message, was informed that the cloak he was asking about had not been left there. The porter asked the waiter to look carefully at the gold watch, which the gentleman had just given him to produce as a token. On examination it was found not to be gold, but only pewter lacquered. The porter then went back to where he had left the box, only to discover no sign of the box or the gang.

He knew that he would be in severe trouble with his master if he went to explain what had happened. In order to try and present a more plausible excuse for returning empty-handed, he rolled himself in the mud and then went home, saying he had been knocked down and robbed of the goods. The owner of the box went to Wild, and repeated the story as told by his servant. Wild knew better, told him he had been deceived as to the manner in which the trunk was lost, and that if he sent for his porter he would soon realise the truth of the matter.

A messenger was sent to fetch him, and, on his arrival Abraham showed him into a room separated from the office only by a slight partition. He told the porter that his master had just come to see them about the missing box, and needed more information about the robbery. What kind of people were the thieves, and how did they come to take the box away. The porter told him that two or three fellows had knocked him down, and then took the box away. Abraham answered that if they knocked him down, there was little chance of the property being recovered, since if they were tried and found guilty of such an offence they would probably be hanged. It was vital that they knew the truth, and if he persisted in refusing, he could rest assured they would find out by some other means. Did he not recall something about a token; was he not asked to fetch a cloak from a tavern; and did he not produce a gold watch as a token to induce the waiter to deliver it? Astonished that Abraham should know absolutely everything already, the porter thought he must have some kind of supernatural powers, and knew it was pointless in holding anything back.

One of the villains involved lived in Wild's old house in Cock Alley, near Cripplegate. Wild and Abraham went there at once, and on arriving at the door they overheard a heated argument between a man and his wife, during which the man declared that he would set out for Holland the next day. At this they forced open the door and Wild, saying he was going to prevent him from making the voyage, took him into custody and conducted him to the Compter. Next day the goods were returned to the owner. Wild was given a handsome reward, and managed to procure the discharge of the thief.

At this stage in his life, he was cautious enough not to run unnecessary risks. In January 1718 two women, Margaret Dodwell and Alice Wright, went to Wild's house, seeking a private interview with him. He noticed that one of them was expecting a child, and imagined she might want to be able to name a father when the time came, for he saw it as part of his business to procure persons to stand in the place of the real fathers of children born 'in consequence of illicit commerce'. When she was shown into another room, Dodwell told him that he had not come to inform him of any loss, but rather that he wanted to find something. If he would follow his advice, he (Wild) would be able to acquire at least a thousand pounds, perhaps many times that amount.

Needless to say Wild was interested, and the woman continued that he must get hold of two or three men who would undertake to rob a house in Wormwood Street, near Bishopsgate. This house was kept by a cane chair maker, John Cooke, who had a lodger, an elderly and extremely wealthy maiden lady, who kept her money in a box in her apartment, and had just gone into the country to collect some more. One of the men had to find an opportunity of getting into the shop in the evening, and concealing himself in a sawpit there. He then intended to let his companions in when the family had gone to bed. In order to accomplish the robbery it would be particularly necessary to secure two stout apprentices, and a boy to lie in the garret. Whatever happened, no murder was to be committed.

At this point Wright entered the conversation, saying that when people engaged in such matters, they had to manage as well as they could, in order to provide for their own safety. Dodwell then continued, saying that once the boys had been secured, there would be no difficulty in getting possession of the old lady's money as she had gone away, and her room was under that where the boys slept. Mr Cooke slept in the bedroom facing that of the old lady; he was a man of some courage, and it would probably be necessary to knock him on the head. As he always kept money on the premises, it would be easy enough to go through his drawers. A woman and a child lay under the room belonging to the old lady, and it was important that they should not be subjected to any violence.

Wild listened carefully to their proposal, then took the women into custody, and lodged them in Newgate. He would probably have had no pangs of conscience in being party to such a scheme, but suspected that it might have been designed to draw him into a snare. Dodwell had lived five months in Mr Cooke's house, and, though she paid no rent, he was too generous to turn her out. Wild prosecuted Dodwell and Wright for a misdemeanour, they appeared in court, were found guilty and each was sentenced each to six months' imprisonment.

Another thief who was not prepared to do Wild's bidding to the letter, but who was fortunate enough to live to tell the tale, was John Butler. After an interview with a client Wild had made notes in his book about a gold watch, a quantity of fine lace, and other property of considerable value, stolen by Butler from a house at Newington Green. Instead of coming to Wild to report on the proceeds of his robbery, Butler decided he was going to give up thieving, but it did not stop him from intending to live on the proceeds of his ill-gotten gains. Angry at being excluded what he saw as his rightful share, Wild determined to pursue every possible means for subjecting him to the power of justice. Learning that Butler was lodging at a public house in Bishopsgate Street, Wild went to the house early one morning. Butler heard him coming up the stairs, jumped out of the window of his room, climbed over the wall of the yard, and went into the street. Wild broke open the door of the room, only to find that his intended quarry had escaped. In the meantime Butler had run into the first house where he saw an open door, and went into the kitchen where some women were doing the washing. He told them he was being pursued by a bailiff, and they advised him to conceal himself in the coal hole.

Wild was wise to the ways of such people trying to elude him. He came out of the alehouse, saw a shop open on the opposite side of the road and asked the master, a dyer, whether a man had recently come and taken refuge in his house. The dyer answered no, as he had not left his shop more than a minute since it had been opened. Wild then went to the house, asked for permission to search the premises, and this was granted. He asked the women if they knew whether a man had taken shelter in the house, and they said no. When he told them the man he sought was a thief, they said he would find him in the coal hole. Wild and his attendants fetched a candle and searched there, then the whole house, but in vain. He decided that the villain must have escaped into the street, but the dyer said that would have been impossible. If he had entered, he must still be in the house, for he had not left the shop, and no man could go onto the street without being noticed. They would have to search the cellar again, and they were rewarded when the dyer checked a large vessel which he regularly used in his business, and found Butler inside. Wild asked him how he had disposed of the goods he stole from Newington Green, told him he had been extremely ungrateful, and declared that he should certainly be hanged.

Butler told Wild to go to his lodging, and look behind the head of the bed, where he would find something for his time and trouble. Wild went there and found a sum of money. However, as Butler had been apprehended in such a public manner, Wild was legally obliged to take him before a magistrate, who committed him for trial. He was tried in the next sessions at the Old Bailey, but Wild managed to ensure that the evidence given against him was not too serious. Instead of being condemned to death, Butler escaped with a sentence to transportation.

Another time Wild was at an inn at Smithfield, when he saw a large trunk in the yard. Imagining that it must have contained property of value, he hastened home, and instructed Jeremiah Rann, one of the thieves he employed on a regular basis, to carry it away. Rann was reckoned one of the most dexterous thieves in London. He dressed himself as a porter, and took the trunk away without being molested. The owner, Mr Jarvis, a whipmaker, soon discovered his loss and applied to Wild, who returned him the goods for a fee of ten guineas. Later Wild and Rann fell out, and when Rann carried out a robbery Wild saw that he was caught, convicted and found guilty. On the day before he was due to be hanged, Rann sent for Jarvis to explain the full story behind the trunk. Wild was threatened with prosecution by Jarvis, but saved by Rann's execution.

As Wild brought so many criminals to justice, admittedly mainly as they had been 'disloyal' to him, the authorities were prepared to tolerate him. On the whole, he had not been affected much by the Transportation Act of 1718. Some of the authorities thought he was being shameless in his activities as receiver and thief-taker, and behaving more boldly than ever, while many of the thieves were appalled at his hypocrisy, though it was not in their interests to speak out against him. Success had surely gone to his head, and he felt assured of his ability to exploit the system and get away with it. Another plausible explanation was that he regarded himself as untouchable and with good reason, being in league with some of the judiciary and with certain high-ranking City officials of the day. It was in their personal interest not to expose the degree to which they were involved with or implicated in dubious schemes themselves. Furthermore most of the magistrates knew that it made sense for them to use Wild for evidence, in a period of mounting anxiety about violent crime and gang activity, as he was a necessary evil. Over and over again he showed no scruples in turning over any of his former associates to the authorities. In a way the act strengthened Wild's hand rather than weakening it, as it made it harder for thieves to fence their goods except through Wild.

On the grounds that his efforts had resulted in more than sixty criminals being led to the gallows, and that he had spent five years apprehending and convicting felons who had returned from transportation before their time, all for no reward, in January 1724 he petitioned the Lord Mayor for the Freedom of the City. It could hardly be denied that he had made the streets safer, by clearing away many notorious gangs. Many of the wealthy London classes were impressed with him, as he had consistently returned their stolen goods and accounts of criminals he had rounded up appeared in the papers every week. They saw him as their best, and perhaps even their only, defence against the crimewave of the time. His petition was thought to have been adjourned, but he was paid a handsome sum by way of gratuity.

By now his battles with thieves were making excellent press. Never slow to seize any opportunity for self-advertisement, he would approach the newspapers with accounts of his good deeds, and the editors passed them on to a concerned but eager readership. Typical of these was a report from the Weekly Journal, 13 June 1719, presenting him as a noble agent of law enforcement:

Jonathan Wild, the British Thief-Taker, going down last week into Oxfordshire with a Warrant from the Lord Chief Justice to apprehend two notorious Highwaymen, who infested the country, met them within a few miles of Oxford on the road. But they hearing of his design met him, and one of them fired a pistol at him: but Jonathan having on the old Proverb for Armour, received no Hurt, and then he discharged a Pistol at them, which wounded one of them so terribly that his life is in great danger: the other was pursued and taken and committed to Oxford Gaol, and Jonathan has given Security to appear the next Assizes to justify his Conduct.

In July and August 1724 the papers carried accounts of his heroic efforts in collecting over twenty members of the Carrick Gang, a group of Irish immigrants, with an £800 reward. When one of the gang, Joseph Blake,* was released, Wild pursued him and had him arrested on 'further information'. To the public this seemed like a relentless defence of order, though it was really no more than a method of gang warfare masquerading as national service. Most people saw in Wild a true public benefactor, a courageous hunter of criminals and breaker of gangs. Between 1721 and 1723 he had been instrumental in destroying four other large gangs in London that between them comprised the hard core of the London underworld, and for the next two years highwaymen avoided the area. Surviving records reveal no instances of any highwayman being convicted or hanged at Tyburn between 1723 and Wild's death two years later, largely as no highwaymen found it possible to operate in London without his 'protection'. His stock had never been higher, and no less a body that the Privy Council used to consult him regularly over the best means of combating the dangerous increase in lawlessness. His 'Office for the Recovery of Lost and Stolen Property' was by now almost a national institution, the Scotland Yard of its day. Newspapers such as the Universal Journal would put 'From Jonathan Wild's at the Old Bailey' as a heading to their weekly crime reports.

Advertisements for his apparent public benefactions, such as the following from the *Daily Post*, 2 November 1724, continued to appear:

Lost, the 1st of October, a black shagreen Pocket-Book, edged with Silver, with some Notes of Hand. The said Book was lost in the Strand, near the Fountain Tavern, about 7 or 8 o'clock at Night. If any Person will bring the aforesaid Book to Mr Jonathan Wild, in the Old Bailey, he shall have a Guinea reward.

Reading between the lines, it is apparent that Wild already had the pocket-book in question, and was offering to return it to its owner for a fee. The reference to 'notes of hand' implied that he already knew who the owner was, and as the Fountain Tavern was a notorious brothel, some measure of blackmail was implicit.

Wild's remarkable run of success was too good to last. Had he remained satisfied with this way of dealing, in all probability he might have gone to his grave in peace. But in his sheer greed he overreached himself, and did not appreciate the virtue of stopping while he was ahead. Instead of keeping to this safe method, he eventually began taking the goods into his own custody, giving those who stole them what he

*See p. 74

thought a satisfactory recompense, and then making any bargain with the loser that he was able to negotiate, sending the porter himself, and taking without ceremony whatever money had been given him for his trouble.

He still did not see fit to observe much discretion with regard to his thief-taking, but on the contrary he was now carrying on his activities more openly and publicly than ever. As if to try and compensate for this in the public eye, he seemed to double his efforts in apprehending thieves, and brought many of the most notorious amongst them to the gallows. That he himself had trained many of them in the art of thieving, and given them instructions and encouragement to take the road to perdition, troubled not his conscience for a moment – if he had one. The day of reckoning would soon come.

The Strand, early nineteenth century

CHAPTER FIVE

Burridge and Hawes

One of Wild's most notorious disciples was William Burridge. Born in West Haden, Northamptonshire, he was a former carpenter's apprentice. Extremely fit and strong, as a young man he had often exercised in wrestling and cudgel-playing for which he was renowned in the locality at wakes and fairs. A lawless youth, during adolescence he was continually running away from his parents, stealing to support himself, until his father decided to wash his hands of him. Realising he was out of control, his friends advised him to go to sea and join a man-o'-war, as that might be the making of an honest man of him. He joined a squadron which was about to sail for Spain under the command of Commodore Cavendish, and was present during an engagement with the Spaniards in Cadiz Bay, when his behaviour proved exemplary and he was praised for his courage under fire. This had the worst possible effect on the impressionable young man, for now he thought himself more worthy of command than most of the officers on the ship, and resented having to take orders from them. This relieved them from the obligation of showing him any kindness, which they would otherwise perhaps have done in consideration of his gallant behaviour against the enemy.

Leaving the naval service, he returned to England and became a highwayman, committed many robberies on the road to Hampstead, on Finchley Common, and in the Hammersmith area. When he first began robbing, he promised himself he would retire when he had made enough money to support himself, but as he found this less lucrative than he had expected, he decided he would join Wild's gang, finding this was a more remunerative way of pursuing such an activity than on his own. After being seized and held in custody for another burglary he escaped, and regularly gave evidence against others at the Old Bailey, a number of whom ended up at Tyburn for their crimes. At one stage he fled to Lincolnshire in order to avoid justice, stole a bay gelding and brought it to London, intending to sell it at Smithfield market. The owner sent a full description of it to London, and Burridge was seen riding on it through the street. When a small party was on the point of arresting him he produced a brace of pistols, threatening instant death to anyone who came near him. He successfully eluded his pursuers for a while but was eventually captured in Mayfair, and held in custody at Newgate. On his trial at the Old Bailey, a man and a woman swore that they had seen him purchase the horse. As there were considerable differences in minor details between their stories, the court decided that they had been hired to pervert the course of justice, and the judge ordered them to be taken into custody for perjury.

While under sentence of death, Burridge seemed to be repenting for his crimes. He and five others went to the gallows at Tyburn on 14 March 1722. Before his execution he delivered a farewell address to the crowds, warning them to be obedient to their parents and masters, and to beware of the crime of debauching young women, which had led him to ruin. He was aged about thirty-four.

Another member of Wild's criminal network was Nathaniel Hawes, born in 1701, son of a grazier from Norfolk, who died when the was about a year old. Later he pretended that he had been defrauded of a greater part of his father's effects which rightfully belonged to him. As a young man he was apprenticed to an upholsterer in London, with whom he stayed for about four years, before he fell in with disreputable company and took to stealing money from his master. After being caught he was tried for robbery at the Old Bailey and convicted of stealing 39s. Although sentenced to seven years' transportation, he was pardoned by the Court on the grounds of youth.

This lucky escape was not enough to stop him from going back to his old ways. He returned to a gang who passed much of their time in drinking, gaming and whoring, not to say more robbery. A hasty temper made him behave with great boldness on such occasions, and gave him a fearsome reputation amongst the gang for which he was extravagantly praised until he began to see himself as a kind of latter-day Don Quixote. He spent much of his time with another noted robber of the day, Richard James, and between them they carried out many of their activities on the Oxford Road, where they took money from passengers, and often subjected them to much violence in the process.

Before long he believed himself to be invincible, and thought that no escapade was beyond him. It was nothing for him when on his own to rob a coach full of gentlemen, to stop two or three persons on the highway at a time, or to steal from waggons in a line as they came on the Oxford Road to London. At length he was caught and committed to New Prison, on suspicion of robbing two gentlemen in a chaise coming from Hampstead. Here he found that he had probably met his match, as it seemed a difficult institution from which to escape. Among his fellow captives were a man and a woman who had been committed for shoplifting. Of the three, the woman seemed more prepared to try and escape from the premises than the other two. The man with her said it would be impracticable, while Hawes boasted that though he had broken open many a prison in his day, he feared this one would be beyond him.

When the woman asked him if he was brave enough to try, he assured her that there was nothing he would not attempt in order to regain his freedom. Not to be outdone, the other man said that if he could see any chance of getting them out, there was nobody with a better pair of hands for such a job than himself. The woman then said that they needed to raise as much money between them as they could in order to keep a very good fire in their cell. Hawes admitted that a fire would be most convenient as the weather was very cold, but he could not understand why lighting one would bring them any closer to their liberty, unless she had some plan to set the whole gaol alight. She sternly told him that all he had to do was to follow her directions, and help her to get some faggots and coals. By the following morning, she promised, they would be out of the place. Her air of self-assurance was so evident that Hawes and the other man decided there was nothing to be lost by obeying her. They kept back one shilling each, but laid out all the rest of their money on combustible material for the fire, and liquor.

Despite her earlier confidence, the woman's mood soon gave way to an appearance of dejection, and neither of the men seemed to have any ideas about escaping. Suddenly she asked if anybody could fetch her a poker or some similar instrument. A fellow prisoner told her that if she gave him twopence, he would bring her one of the old bars that had been taken out of the window when the new ones were fitted. She handed over the money and he delivered the promised item. A little later the keepers locked them up, barred and bolted the doors, and left them until the next morning.

Once she was sure they were no longer being watched, she told Hawes and their companion that it was time they got to work. Putting her hands in her pockets and shaking her petticoats, she produced two small bags of tools which fell on the ground. Next she pointed out to them a large stone at the corner of the roof which was morticed into two others, one above and the other below. After they had picked all the mortar from between them, she heated the bar red hot in the fire, and putting it to the sockets into which the irons that held the stones were fastened with lead, it quickly loosened them. They then used the bars as a crow, and by about 2.00 next morning they had managed to get themselves out, and opened themselves a suitable passage through which they could escape into the street. After this the woman made them fasten the iron bar strongly at the angle where the three stones met. Next she pulled off her stays, unrolled from the top of her petticoats four yards of strong cord, fastened the noose on the iron and threw the other end out over the wall, in order to give them an easy descent. The men were delighted and surprised at their good fortune, and out of gratitude to the woman, helped her to the top of the wall first, letting her get away safely before they left themselves.

While he was in Newgate, Hawes made several unsavoury friends, and shortly after he was free again he joined a group of thieves acting under Wild's direction. He went into partnership with one, John James, and they committed several robberies together. For a while theis proved successful, but after one spell of thieving they quarrelled, fell out on the division of the goods, and decided to go their own separate ways. Later Hawes was anxious lest James might seek revenge by giving evidence against him, and acting on the principle that who struck first would win, he applied to Wild, and informed against his old acquaintance. James was taken into custody, tried and executed. However Hawes did not get everything his own way, as the Court also sentenced him to prison. He made a special request to be taken to the New Prison instead of Newgate, as he suspected that the inmates of the latter were threatening to murder him for having given evidence against James. A recently passed Act for the More Effectual Conviction of Highwaymen made the evidence of accomplices legally admissible, but the person or persons giving evidence could not claim liberty unless two or more of his accomplices were convicted. As only one accomplice, James, had been convicted, Hawes could still be (and was) sent to prison.

Soon after he was committed Hawes and another felon escaped, and entering into another partnership committed several robberies, mainly on the road between Hackney and Shoreditch. Once again this connection lasted but a short time as, true to form, he and his fellow robber fell out in a dispute over dividing their ill-gotten gains. Soon after this Hawes went on his own to Finchley Common, where he encountered Richard Hall, a gentleman riding to town, pointed a pistol at his breast and ordered him to dismount at once, that he might search him for his money. The gentleman offered him four shillings, on which Hawes swore the most horrid oaths, and threatened instant death if he did not immediately submit. Hall dismounted from his horse, and at once seized the pistol, which he snatched from the hand of the robber, telling him to expect death if he did not agree to surrender himself. Hawes, who was now as terrified as he had been insolent, did not put up any fight. The driver of a cart was approaching just at that moment, and Hawes was captured, taken to London, and held in Newgate.

For this robbery he was detected and apprehended, convicted and sentenced to death. When he was first placed in custody, he declared with a considerable display of vanity that he would merit a greater reputation by the boldness of his behaviour than any other highwayman who had died these seven years. At the time he was seized, a good suit of clothes was taken from him, and he took grave offence because, he said, it would be impossible for him to appear like a gentleman at the sessions-house. Inordinately proud of his appearance, he told the court that he would refuse to plead when he was arraigned and sent for trial unless they were returned to him. 'The people,' he announced, 'who apprehended me, seized a suit of fine clothes, which I intended to have gone to the gallows in; and unless they are returned I will not plead, for no one shall say that I was hanged in a dirty shirt and ragged coat.' He insisted that he would die, as he had lived, like a gentleman; and maintained that the Court had formerly been a place of Justice, but now it was become a place of injustice; that he had not the slightest doubt that in due course they would receive a severer sentence than that which they had just pronounced upon him. As to the manner of his departing this life, he 'made no question of dying with the same resolution with which he had often beheld death, and would leave the world with the same courage with which he had lived in it'.

The Court answered that it was simply not in their power to hand back the clothes he demanded back. When he persisted in remaining silent, the judge at last ordered that the sentence of the press should be read to him. He was taken from the courtroom, laid on his back, and sustained a load of 250 lb weight about seven minutes after which the Judge from the Bench addressed him:

> The equity of the Law of England, more tender of the lives of its subjects than any other in the world, allows no person to be put to death, either unheard or without the positive proof against him of the fact whereon he stands charged; and that proof, too, must be such as shall satisfy twelve men who are his equals, and by whose verdict he is to be tried. And surely no method can be devised fuller than this is, as well of compassion, as of Justice. But then it is required that the person to be tried shall aver his innocence by pleading Not Guilty to his indictment, which contains the charge. You have heard that which the grand jury have found against you. You see here twelve honest men ready to enquire impartially into the evidence that shall be given against you. The Court, such is the humanity of our constitution, is counsel for you as you are a prisoner. What hinders then, that you should submit to so fair, so equal a trial; and wherefore will you, by a brutish obstinacy, draw upon you that heavy judgement which the Law has appointed for those who seem to have lost the rational faculties of men?

When some of his companions said jestingly that he had chosen the pressing because the Court would not let him have a good suit of clothes to be hanged in, he replied that as he had lived with the character of the boldest fellow of his profession he was resolved to die with it, and leave his memory to be admired by all the gentlemen of the road in succeeding ages. At length he could not bear the pain of the weight any longer, and begged to be taken back to the courtroom. Although he pleaded not guilty, the evidence against him was overwhelming, and he was convicted and sentenced to death.

The bruises on his chest continued to give him so much discomfort during what little time he had left on earth. He confessed to all the crimes he could remember being responsible for, and seemed very keen to acquit some innocent persons who were currently languishing in prison for, or had been suspected of, some of the misdemeanours he and his gang had committed. After receiving the Sacrament, he went to his execution with all due dignity on 21 December 1721 at Tyburn, aged twenty.

CHAPTER SIX

Levey, Oakey and Flood

John Levey, Richard Oakey and Matthew Flood were a trio of thieves who worked for Wild, sometimes together, and they all went to the gallows as one. John Levey's original family name was Levee; his father had come over to England with King Charles II at the Restoration, and taught French to several people in court circles, including some of the King's natural children. He kept a large boarding school in Pall Mall, and later set up in business as a wine merchant. When this failed he and the family settled in Holland. His son John went to sea with a captain of a man-o'-war and was on board the Essex when Sir George Byng, later Viscount Torrington, engaged the Spaniards at Messina. On returning to England, he studied book-keeping.

From this he soon drifted into a life of villainy, but at least had some sense of family honour. To avoid bringing disgrace on their good name, he took to calling himself John Junks instead. He and his companions began by robbing in quite a gentlemanly fashion, by putting a hat into the coach and asking the passengers to contribute as they thought fit, being always contented with whatever was given. They were so civil that Blake and Levey, once robbing a woman on her own in a coach, found she had a basketful of buns and cakes with her. Levey took some of them, while Blake proceeded to search her for money, but found none. The woman scratched him and called him several rude names, slapping him hard in the face as she did so. Fortunately for her, they merely laughed before withdrawing, leaving her unmolested.

When they learnt from other members of the criminal fraternity that large sums could be made with ease on Blackheath, they decided to go and try their luck there. Accordingly they set out as six horsemen well armed and mounted. After they had been on the heath for about six hours without meeting a single unwary traveller, and continuing this hollow pursuit for the next three or four days, they agreed they might as well try somewhere else in future. In the following December, Levey and another man robbed a butcher on horseback on the road coming from Hampstead. The man had told them he had sold two lambs there, and Levey's companion said immediately that as the price of lambs was 14s apiece, he would have 28s on him. They threatened him until he gave them the money, and for good measure they took his coat as well. They would probably have tried to relieve him of even more, but Levey suddenly saw a coach coming their way, and persuaded his associates to be content with what they had for the time being.

Levey rarely used violence on anyone in his robberies. The exception was when he accosted a Mr Betts, who put up a fight and struck him three or four blows on the head. Levey retaliated, and with one blow of his pistol struck his eye out. One night, while Blake and Matthew Flood were accompanying Levey, they stopped the chariot of Mr Young, whose evidence had sent Molony and Carrick to the gallows. Blake called out to lay hold, and Flood stopped the horses, then Levey went into the coach and took from Mr Young a gold watch and chain, with Oakey assisting him. They robbed also Colonel Cope, who was in the same coach, of his gold watch, chain and ring, and 22s. Levey said it would have been a very easy matter for the gentleman to have taken him, as he had gone into the coach unarmed, and his companions were on the other side of the hedge. However they gave him the things very readily, and it was hard to say who behaved themselves most civilly one towards the other, the gentlemen or he. One of them asked to have a cornelian ring returned, which Levey was prepared to do, but his companions would not let him.

As they were going home afterwards, they met a poor man on horseback. Despite the considerable sum they had just taken, they turned out of the road, carried him behind two haycocks as the moon was shining so light, and found that his entire worldly wealth amounted to a paltry two shillings. The others in the gang immediately said they ought to tie him up and beat him. But when he told them that he was very sick and begged them to treat him gently, Levey prevailed with them not only to put him on his horse again, but also to give him back his two shillings, and lead him into the road where they left him.

Levey, Flood and Oakey were soon apprehended, while Blake secured his freedom by turning evidence. They were convicted at the next sessions at the Old Bailey, and sentenced to death. Levey behaved himself while under condemnation very seriously and modestly, though before that time, he had acted too much the bravo, from the mistaken opinion that it made him appear braver and more resolute than the rest. As the moment of his execution came closer he changed, 'and applied himself with great seriousness and attention to prayers and other duties becoming a person in his condition'. At the gallows he strongly objected to his hands being tied, and the cap pulled over his face. It was all to no avail, and he was obliged by the executioner to submit as the others did. He was aged about twenty-seven.

Richard Oakey was a tailor's apprentice before he turned to thieving. First he was a pickpocket preying on women, which he said he did in a manner peculiar to himself. He used to dress like a gentleman in order to avoid suspicion, then passed by the woman whom he intended to rob, took up their upper petticoat and cut off the pocket at once, tripping them down at the same time. Then he stepped softly on the other side of the way, walked on and thus managed to avoid suspicion. Later he said that while he was a boy, he had committed several hundred robberies this way. Later he made use of a woman to assist him, by pushing his victims against the wall, while he took the opportunity of cutting their pockets. At other times this woman came behind other unwary people as they were about to cross the road, and catching them by the arm, cried out, 'There's a coach will run over ye'; while Oakey took advantage of the distraction to whip off their pocket.

One woman who had helped him in his thieving for some time, had a difference with him one night at an alehouse. He hit out and beat her, she swore at him and he continued to attack her more viciously. At length she roared out 'Murder', which proved a self-fulfilling prophecy. By now she was so badly beaten that she died from the blows, but the people of the house were at pains to conceal the crime in order to avoid any scandal, and buried her privately. Oakey now had to go on his old way by himself, and he followed the practice of snatching off pockets without a partner. Soon he became one of the most dexterous in his profession. A little later he became acquainted with several housebreakers, who persuaded him to follow their course of life, which they thought more profitable than stealing of pockets. In the first attempt they were successful; but the second, in which two others were also involved, was breaking open a shop in Southwark near the Mint, where they stole a quantity of calimancoes or pieces of good quality glossy woollen fabric, worth over £20. Oakey was apprehended and impeached his accomplices, who were convicted at Kingston Assizes. One was hanged and the other transported on his evidence.

Deterred from the thoughts of housebreaking by this adventure, he returned for a while to his old employment, and then became acquainted with a man called Will the Sailor. Will, who wore a sword, used to affront persons in the streets, and provoke them till they stripped to fight with him, and then Oakey used to decamp with their clothes. They soon quarrelled, and parted; Will grew tired of his companion, or of the dangerous trade which he was engaged in, certain it is that he left it off, and got again out of England on ship-board. Oakey then took to thieving with several others including Hawes, Milksop, Lincoln, Reading, Wilkinson, but ended up turning evidence against them and before long they all went to the gallows.

By now an accomplished thief, Oakey joined Wild's gang, which at this time included John Levey, Matthew Flood, and Blake, with whom he continued until his crimes and theirs brought them together to the gallows. These men were for some time the terror of travellers near London. Among other robberies, they stopped a coach between Camberwell and London, in which were five men and a woman. The men said they would deliver their money, but begged they would not search, as the lady was with child. Holding a hat, Blake collected the money the passengers put into it, which appeared on first glance to be a large sum, but closer examination revealed that most of the coins were halfpennies. The gang suspected that Blake must have defrauded them, as it was by no means the first time he had cheated on his fellow thieves. Later they were angry with themselves when they learned that they had failed to make a thorough search of the coach, and the passengers had been carrying about £300 between them.

A while after this Oakey, Levey, Flood, and Blake stopped Colonel Cope and Mr Young, in a carriage, on their return from Hampstead, and robbed them of their watches, rings, and money. Information of this robbery was sent to Wild, who had the parties apprehended. Blake gave evidence against them and they were tried, convicted, sentenced, and ordered for execution. After condemnation Oakey's behaviour was such as became his condition, getting up in the night to pray so often and manifesting all the signs of a sincere repentance. He said that what troubled him more than all his other offences put together was his burning a will that he found with some money and rings in a pocket which he had cut from a lady's side, an action which proved highly detrimental to the owner. They were executed at Tyburn on 23 February 1723.

Matthew Flood was the son of a man who kept the Clink Prison in the parish of St Mary Overys, who had given him as good an education as possible, and bound him as apprentice to one Mr Williams, a lighterman. Until 1745 the Clink Prison was at the corner of Maid Lane, Southwark, and originally used as a house of detention for heretics and offenders against the bishop of Winchester, whose palace stood nearby. Unfortunately Flood, like so many others, fell into the wrong company. He spent a mere three months as part of the gang before the Hampstead robbery which led them all to conviction. Once he had been tried and sentenced to death for his part in the crime his behaviour was very penitent and modest, and he was not vain or foolish enough to place any great faith in the hopes his friends gave him of a reprieve. Addressing the public from the gallows, he said he was more particularly concerned for a robbery he had committed on a woman in Cornhill, not only because he took from her a good many guineas which were in her pocket, but that at the same time also he had taken a will which he burnt, and which he feared would be more to her prejudice than the loss of her money. Oakey was about twenty-five years old at his death, Matthew Flood a year or two younger.

CHAPTER SEVEN

Sheppard, Blake and Bellamy

Two of Wild's most notorious associates went to the gallows in 1724. He bore some responsibility for their being brought to justice, but their executions helped to weaken what had been his previously almost unassailable position and ultimately contributed towards dragging him down to a similar fate. At the time London political life was experiencing a crisis of public confidence. Since the South Sea Bubble had burst in 1720, a collapse in the stock market which resulted in a wave of bankruptcies for people from all walks of life, the public was less tolerant of corruption in high places, and authority figures were viewed with scepticism. General alarm about outbreaks of mohocking, or upper-class hooliganism, riots by weavers and apprentices, rumours of Hell-Fire Clubs, treasonable conspiracies and imminent Jacobite invasions, all contributed towards an air of general unease.

In April 1724 the most famous housebreaker of the era, Jack Sheppard, was apprehended by one of Wild's men, James 'Hell-and-Fury' Sykes, for a burglary he had committed in Clare Market on 5 February. The exploits of Jack Sheppard, master housebreaker and escaper, were the talk of all ranks of society. Books and pamphlets were written about him, while a contemporary pantomime at Drury Lane, Harlequin Sheppard, and a three-act farce, The Prison-Breaker, were both based on the story of his adventures. Many songs and glees referred to his prowess, and clergymen preached sermons about him. Sir James Thornhill, Serjeant-Painter to the Crown, and the artist who had decorated the dome of St Paul's Cathedral, painted his portrait while he was in the condemned cell, and engravings in mezzotinto were made. This inspired a few verses from an anonymous poet:

> Thornhill, 'tis thine to gild with fame
> The obscure, and raise the humble name;
> To make the form elude the grave,
> And Sheppard from oblivion save.

Though life in vain the wretch implores,
An exile on the farthest shores,
Thy pencil brings a kind reprieve,
And bids the dying robber live.
This piece to latest time shall stand,
And show the wonders of thy hand:
Thus former masters graced their name,
And gave egregious robbers fame.
Apelles Alexander drew,
Caesar is to Aurelius due;
Cromwell in Lely's works doth shine,
And Sheppard, Thornhill, lives in thine.

John, or Jack, Sheppard was born on 4 March 1702 in White Row, Spitalfields. His father Thomas, a carpenter, had another son, also named Thomas, who was also convicted at the Old Bailey for theft. Thomas the elder died while the boys were young, and they were brought up by their mother Mary. He became apprentice to a cane chair-maker, and after his mother died, he was employed as a servant by William Kneebone, a woollen draper, at the sign of the Angel on the north side of the Strand, opposite St Mary's Church. Kneebone showed considerable kindness to the boy, helped him to improve his writing and knowledge of mathematics, and in April 1717 apprenticed him to Owen Wood, a carpenter in Drury Lane. He was a hard worker, and soon had the reputation of being a talented worker of whom much was expected.

However, in 1722 Joseph Hayne, a button-mould maker who lived next door to Sheppard's master, gave up his trade to take the Black Lion alehouse in Lewkenor's Lane, and he encouraged Sheppard and other apprentices to patronise the house. At the Black Lion Sheppard was introduced to 'a train of vices as before I was altogether a stranger to'. He became acquainted with some abandoned women, among them Elizabeth Lyon, otherwise known as 'Edgworth Bess' from the town of Edgworth, where she was born (though some sources say it was Edgware). Nothing was known of her early life, or even whether Lyon was a maiden or married name. She may have been the same as one Elizabeth Miller, convicted at the Old Bailey and branded in the hand in October 1721 for stealing a piece of silk and five yards of cambric from the house of John Davenport, where she was lodging, in the parish of St Peter Westcheap, London, though her main claim to fame is as Sheppard's mistress. Her behaviour was thought shocking even by most of his companions, who were long hardened to every kind of vice, but she soon established a hold over him, and it was she who initiated him into making money by fair means or foul. Physically she was a large, well-built masculine woman, while he was slight of stature, though very strong for his size. He was a heavy drinker, and both of them used to fight each other quite viciously when he was drunk. They often argued and sometimes went for weeks at a time barely on speaking terms. Nevertheless they could not do without each other for long, and she accompanied him in many of his robberies and escapes.

While Sheppard continued to work as a carpenter, he frequently committed robberies in the houses where he was employed, stealing small but valuable items such as tankards, spoons and silver, all of which he took to Bess. His first known theft was from the Rummer tavern at Charing Cross, where he had been sent on an errand for his master, but ending up stealing two silver spoons instead. In August 1723, after more thefts, usually from houses where he had been working, he absconded from his master and drifted into a life of professional crime. Before long he was committing burglaries with Bess and his brother Thomas. The latter had recently been indicted at the Old Bailey for two petty offences, convicted and branded on the hand, and then decided to throw in his lot with his seemingly more successful brother and Bess. Together they broke open an alehouse in Southwark and carried off a large amount of money and property. Jack generously let his brother keep it all, and soon after gave him a fine suit of clothes, so that Thomas would not let the family name down by appearing in 'unbecoming style' as the famous Mr Sheppard's brother among the fair damsels of Drury Lane.

The fraternal thieving partnership did not last long. Their next venture, in February 1724, was to break open the shop of Mrs Cook, a linen-draper in Clare Market, and carried off goods worth £55. Less than a fortnight afterwards they stole some articles from the house of Mr Phillips, in Drury Lane. While going to sell some of the goods stolen at Mrs Cook's, Tom Sheppard was apprehended and committed to Newgate. Worried that he might go to the gallows, he promptly informed on his brother and Bess. Jack was arrested as a result of his brother's information, and committed by Justice Parry to the Roundhouse for further questioning. The house was not strong enough to hold him, and he escaped almost at once by breaking a hole through the roof. It was merely the first of a series of daring and skilful escapes from captivity which would soon make him famous. Meanwhile he vowed vengeance on Tom, who as he said had so basely behaved himself towards so good a brother. There was no honour among thieves, whether they were siblings or merely partners in crime.

Another of Sheppard's associates was a Poll Maggott who had nothing but contempt for him, and shamelessly used him to go and steal money, or anything that might raise funds, for her to spend while she mixed in more congenial company. One night he told her he had pawned the last object he had in the world for half a crown, but she told him dismissively that he was capable of getting his hands on far more than that. She had been in Whitehorse Yard that afternoon and saw Mr Bains, a very well-off piece-broker. He kept his cash in a drawer under the counter, and the shop was full of fine clothes that she would like to wear. A word to the wise was enough, and now she would see how long it would take him to get hold of them for her. At about 1.00 the following morning he went to the house, took up the cellar window bars, entered the shop, stole money and goods worth £22, and took it to her at once. She appeared satisfied with his work, but it was not long before they squandered the entire proceeds.

From the same place he took away a piece of fustian, a particularly fine fabric, which he deposited in his trunk. As Sheppard did not go home that night, nor the following day, Kneebone suspected that he was up to no good. He told Bains of his supicions, the latter checked over his goods, found that the fustian was missing, suspected Sheppard was responsible for its disappearance, and determined to have him taken into custody. When Jack heard about this, he swore that his mother had given him the fustian after buying it for him in Spitalfields, and threatened to prosecute for libel. Intent on protecting her son, the mother declared his story was true, though she was unable to point out the exact place where she had made the purchase. Though he did not believe a word of it, Bains reluctantly agreed that he would let the matter rest for lack of proof.

Kneebone was prepared to give Sheppard the benefit of the doubt on this occasion, and retained his services a little longer, but he continued to associate with disreputable company, often staying out all night. A quarrel with both men led to Sheppard's dismissal, and he threw in with Wild's gang, while taking another carpentry job – with the ultimate aim of robbing his new employer. While employed to assist in repairing the house of a gentleman in Mayfair he took an opportunity of stealing a sum of money, some plate, gold rings and four suits of clothes. Not long after this Bess was apprehended and lodged in the St Giles's roundhouse. He went to visit her, and when the beadle refused to admit him he knocked the man down, broke open the door, and carried her off in triumph, an exploit which acquired him a high degree of credit with other women of abandoned character.

Another notorious felon of the day and companion of Jack Sheppard, James Sykes, commonly known as 'Hell and Fury', met him in St Giles's and invited him into a public house, hoping to receive a reward for apprehending him. While they were drinking, Sykes sent for a constable, who took Jack into custody and had him up before a magistrate, who gave him a cursory examination and sent him to St Giles's Roundhouse. Within three hours he had broken through the roof, and escaped under cover of darkness in the night. A little later, as Sheppard and Benson, another associate, were crossing Leicester Fields, the latter tried to pick a gentleman's pocket of his watch. The man called out, 'a pickpocket!' and a crowd gathered round. Sheppard was taken and lodged in St Ann's Roundhouse, where he was visited next day by Bess, who was detained on suspicion of being one of his accomplices and locked up with him.

Next day they were brought before the magistrate, charged and committed to New Prison, Clerkenwell. As they passed for husband and wife, they were allowed to lodge together in a room known by the name of Newgate Ward. Sheppard was visited by several of his cronies, some of whom brought him some tools so he could try and escape again. Early one morning a few days later, he filed off his fetters. made a hole in the wall, then took an iron bar and a wooden one out of the window. As he would need to descend from a height of about 25 ft he tied a blanket and sheet together, made one them fast to a bar in the window, Bess descended first, and Jack followed her. Having reached the yard, they had still a wall of twenty-two feet high to scale; but climbing up by the locks and bolts of the great gate, they got quite out of the prison, and made a perfect escape.

To his fellow-thieves, Sheppard became a hero overnight once the exploit became common knowledge. A cooper, Charles Grace, asked him if he would take him as an associate in his robberies, as his girlfriend was so extravagant that he could not possibly support her on the profits of his own thefts. Both men made the acquaintance of Anthony Lamb, an apprentice to Mr Carter, a mathematical instrument-maker, near St Clement's Church, and agreed to rob a man who lodged with Lamb's master, Mr Barton. At about 2 a.m. Lamb let the men into the premises, where they stole money and effects to a large amount, while Lamb himself retired to bed to prevent suspicion. Grace and Sheppard then fell out after quarrelling over the division of goods, Sheppard wounded Grace seriously, and all three betrayed one another. They were arrested, but true to form Sheppard soon escaped. He was recaptured and taken into custody, where he confessed everything before a magistrate, and was committed to Newgate.

Lamb was the youngest and most innocent of the trio. He had been duped into taking part, and persuaded several gentlemen who knew him to vouch for his good character. Their influence helped him in having his sentence commuted to transportation to Australia, as well as an order that on his arrival there he should not be sold like the other felons, but left at liberty to provide for himself as well as he could. On the same day Jack's brother Thomas, was indicted for breaking open the dwelling-house of Mary Cook and stealing her goods, convicted and also sentenced to transportation.

By now Sheppard's gang consisted of himself, his brother Tom, Joseph Blake,* Grace, and James 'Hell and Fury' Sykes. Unsure of the safest way of disposing of the goods they had taken, they used William Field, one of Wild's men, as a fence. Sheppard claimed that he was a fellow wicked enough to do anything, but his want of courage permitted him to do nothing except carry on the trade he did, namely selling stolen goods when put into his hands.

Wild asked Sykes, who had done some thieving for him in the past, if he would like to challenge Sheppard to a game of skittles at Redgate's public house near Seven Dials. Sykes accordingly did so, which enabled him to betray Sheppard to a Mr Price, a constable from the parish of St Giles's, and claim the usual £40 reward for giving information leading to the conviction of a felon. The magistrate, Justice Parry, had Sheppard imprisoned overnight on the top floor of St Giles's Roundhouse pending further questioning, but he escaped within three hours by breaking through the timber ceiling and lowering himself to the ground with a rope fashioned from bedclothes. Still wearing irons, he joined the crowd that had been attracted by the sounds of him breaking out. He distracted their attention by pointing to the shadows on the roof

*See p. 74

Jack Sheppard in the Store Room at Newgate

and shouting that he could see the man who had escaped, and then swiftly departed while they were looking the other way.

On 19 May 1724 he was arrested for a second time, caught picking a pocket in Leicester Fields. He was detained overnight in St Ann's Roundhouse in Soho and visited there the next day by Lyon; she was recognised as his wife and locked in a cell with him. They appeared before Justice Walters, who sent them to the New Prison in Clerkenwell, but they escaped from their cell, known as the Newgate Ward, within a matter of days. By 25 May, Whitsun Monday, Sheppard and Bess had filed through their manacles; they removed a bar from the window and used their knotted bed-clothes, Bess's gown and petticoat, to descend to ground level. Finding themselves in the prison yard, they clambered over the 22 ft perimeter wall to freedom.

In summer 1724, Sheppard and Blake went robbing on the Hampstead Road. The latter committed several further burglaries, including one on the house of his former benefactor William Kneebone on the night of 12–13 July. Sheppard and Blake hired a stable near the Horse Ferry, Westminster, and used it as a warehouse for their stolen goods, including the woollen cloth stolen from Mr Kneebone, while they considered the best way to dispose of them. Sheppard and Blake had applied to Field to look at these goods and procure a customer for them, as he assured them that he could sell the goods for a worthwhile price. He promised to look at the goods, and did so – but not in the manner they had intended. In the night he broke open their warehouse, stole everything, and then informed against them to Wild, who could not continue to allow Sheppard to work outside his control and had them apprehended. After Sheppard had a brief foray with Blake as highwaymen on the Hampstead Road on 19 and 20 July, Field informed on Sheppard to Wild. The latter was sure Lyon would know Sheppard's whereabouts, so he plied her with drinks at a brandy shop near Temple Bar until she told him where to find him. Sheppard was arrested a third time at Blake's mother's brandy shop in Rosemary Lane, east of the Tower of London, on 23 July by Wild's henchman, Quilt Arnold, and committed to prison in the City of London. Arnold had been working for Wild since about 1716 as his 'Clerk of the Northern Roads'. Wild told the authorities that the duties of this post involved keeping the Northern Roads clear of thieves, but his real job was to organise crime along them. Sheppard fired a pistol at Arnold but missed.

He was brought to trial at the Old Bailey on 13 August, and charged with several offences, among them breaking and entering the house of William Kneebone and stealing 108 yds of woollen cloth and other articles. Due to lack of evidence he was acquitted on two charges, but Wild had made arrangements for Field and Kneebone, his old master, to present evidence against him on a third charge, namely that of the burglary of Kneebone's house on 12 July. Sheppard was convicted of the Kneebone robbery on 12 August and sentenced to death. His defence rested on the fact that Wild had helped to dispose of part of the goods, and he thought it very hard that he should not share in the punishment. The Court took little notice of what they deemed so insignificant a plea, and sentence was passed upon him. Throughout the proceedings, he behaved 'as a person either stupid or foolish, so far was he from appearing in any degree likely to make the noise he afterwards did'.

On 30 August 1724 a warrant was sent to Newgate for his execution, as well as for several other convicts who were also under sentence of death. In the old Newgate gaol there was a hatch, with large iron spikes, which opened into a dark passage, and from there a few steps led into the condemned hold. The prisoners were allowed to come down to the hatch to speak with their friends. Sheppard had been supplied with several tools, and took an opportunity of cutting one of the spikes so it could be easily broken off. That same evening his old accomplices Bess and Poll Maggott came to visit him, bringing some more tools. They took advantage of the fact that some of the keepers were drinking at the other end of the lodge at the time. He either sawed through or broke off the spike, thrust his head and shoulders through the space, the women pulled him out, and he escaped from the hold into the lodge, the prison's reception area.

Disguised in the women's clothing they had also brought with them, he was taken safely out by the lodge door, and took a hackney coach to Blackfriars Stairs. There he boarded a boat up the River Thames to the horse ferry in Westminster, near the warehouse where he hid his stolen goods, and made good his escape. On the following day he went to a public house in Spitalfields, where he sent for an old acquaintance, Mr Page, a butcher in Clare Market, who gave him a frock in which to disguise himself, and suggested he leave the London area for a while. After some consideration they decided to go to Wavendon, Buckinghamshire, where Page had some relations. However they took a dim view of a member of their family bringing such disreputable company with him, and treated Sheppard with such coldness that they returned to London after about a week.

On the night after their return, as they were walking up Fleet Street together, they saw a watchmaker's shop open, with only a boy looking after the premises. Having passed the shop at first, they then thought it too good an opportunity to miss. Sheppard thrust his hand through the window, and stole three watches. Once news of the theft got out, some of Sheppard's old acquaintances warned him that a strict search was being made for him, and he and Page retired to Finchley Common. Page got away, but on 10 September the keepers of Newgate came and seized Sheppard, took him into custody and returned him to what was rapidly becoming familiar territory. He was put into a strongroom, handcuffed, loaded with a heavy pair of irons, and chained to a staple fixed in the floor, but yet again he managed to get out. On 16 September, after a set of tools was found concealed in the rushes of his chair, he was moved to a formidable fourth-storey apartment known as the Castle, where he was isolated from other prisoners and where visitors were carefully watched. He was clapped in leg irons, and chained to two metal staples in the floor to prevent further escape attempts.

Meanwhile Blake was arrested by Wild and his men on 9 October, and Tom, Jack's brother, was transported for robbery the next day. When the new court sessions began on 14 October, Blake was tried the following day, with Field and Wild again giving evidence against him. Their accounts were not consistent with that which they had given at Sheppard's trial, but Blake was convicted.*

Taking advantage of the disturbance, which spread to Newgate Prison next door and continued into the night, Sheppard accomplished his last and most spectacular escape on 15 October, unlocking his handcuffs and removing the chains. Still encumbered by his leg irons, he tried to climb up the chimney, but his path was blocked at first by an iron bar set into the brickwork. It did not take him long to remove the bar, which he used to break through the ceiling into the 'Red Room' above the 'Castle', a room last used some seven years previously to confine aristocratic Jacobite prisoners captured after the Battle of Preston. Still wearing his leg irons as night fell, he broke his way through the locks, bolts, and bars of six strong doors into the prison chapel to make his way on to the roof of Newgate, 60 ft above the ground. He then returned to his cell to get a blanket, climbed back on to the roof of the prison, and used the blanket to reach the roof of an adjacent house, owned by William Bird, a turner, entered it through a garret window, crept down the stairs and out into the street at around

---

*See p. 76

Jack Sheppard in Newgate Gaol, prior to one of his escapes

midnight without disturbing the occupants. After escaping through the streets to the north and west, he went and hid in a cowshed in Tottenham. When he was spotted by the barn's owner, Sheppard told him that he had just escaped from Bridewell Prison, having been imprisoned there for failing to support an apparently non-existent illegitimate son. His leg irons remained in place for several days, until he told the same story to a passing shoemaker and paid him 20s to bring a blacksmith's tools and help him to cut them off. They were subsequently recovered at the lodgings of Catherine Cook, another of his mistresses, in Cranbourn Alley, Leicester Fields.

Sheppard's audacious career on the wrong side of the law was nearly over. He had just one burglary left to commit – on the night of 29-30 October at a pawnbroker's shop in Drury Lane. By the time he was arrested in a Drury Lane brandy shop on 31 October, dressed in the handsome black suit of clothes and gold watch which was one of the pieces he had stolen from Mr Rawlins, he was very drunk, his wits dulled by too much brandy and over-confidence. He was recognised by a boy who knew him well and informed on him, and was probably not fully aware of what was happening to him when justice laid its hand on his shoulder once more.

Not surprisingly his gaolers had learned their lesson, and now went to great lengths to prevent him from making them look foolish by escaping a third time. On this occasion they dared not take their eyes off him or leave him alone a moment. As this incurred them in additional expense, they found a way of paying themselves with the money they took from curious members of the public who flocked to come and see the man, who was England's most notorious prisoner, at 1s 6d a time. It proved a highly lucrative attraction, and by 7 November the turnkeys were said to have earned themselves more than £200 from charging fees to visitors.

He had now become so famous though his exploits that he was visited by great numbers of people, whom he tried to divert by a recital of the particulars of many robberies in which he had been concerned. When any nobleman came to visit him he asked them if they would intercede with the King for a pardon, 'to which he thought that his singular dexterity gave him some pretensions'.

An account of his escapades, written in the first person by Daniel Defoe, recalled this remarkable turn of events:

As my last escape from Newgate, out of the strong room called the Castle, had made a greater noise in the world than any other action of my life, I shall relate every minute circumstance thereof, as far as I am able to remember.

After I had been made a public spectacle of for many days together, with my legs chained together, loaded with heavy irons and stapled down to the floor, I thought it was not altogether impracticable to escape if I could but be furnished with proper implements; but, as every person that came near me was carefully watched, there was no possibility of any such assistance, till one day in the absence of my jailers, looking about the floor, I spied a small nail within reach, and with that, after a little practice, I found the great horse padlock that went from the chain to the staple in the floor might be unlocked, which I did afterward at pleasure; and was frequently about the room and several times slept on the barracks when the keepers imagined I had not been out of my chair. But being unable to pass up the chimney and void of tools, I remained where I was, till being detected in these practices by the keepers, who surprised me one day before I could fix myself to the staple in the manner as they had left me, I showed Mr Pitt, Mr Rouse and Mr Parry my art and before their faces unlocked the padlock with the nail; and, though people have made such an outcry about it, there is scarce a smith in London but what may easily do the same thing. However, this called for a further security of me. Till now, I had remained without handcuffs, but a jolly pair was provided for me.

Mr Kneebone was present when they were put on. I with tears begged his intercession to the keepers to preserve me from those dreadful manacles, telling him my heart was broken and that I should be much more miserable than before. Mr Kneebone could not refrain from shedding tears himself and did use his good offices with the keepers to keep me from them, but all to no purpose. On they went, though at the time I despised them and well knew that with my teeth only I could take them off at pleasure. But this was to lull them into a firm belief that they had effectually frustrated all attempts to escape for the future. The turnkey and Mr Kneebone had not been gone down stairs an hour when I made an experiment and got off my handcuffs, and before they visited me again I put them on and industriously rubbed and fretted the skin on my wrists, making them very bloody, as thinking (if such a thing was possible to be done) to move the turnkeys to compassion, but rather to confirm them in their opinion; but, though this had no effect upon them, it wrought much upon the spectators and drew from them not only much pity but quantities of silver and copper. I wanted a still more useful metal, a crow, a chisel, a file and a saw or two, these weapons being more useful to me than all the mines of Mexico; but there was no expecting any such utensils in my circumstances.

Wednesday the 14th of October the sessions beginning, I found there was not a moment to be lost; and the affair of Jonathan Wild's throat, together with the business at the Old Bailey, having sufficiently engaged the attention of the keepers, I thought then was the time to push. Thursday the 15th at about two in the afternoon, Austin, my old attendant, came to bring my necessaries and brought up four persons, namely, the keeper of Clerkenwell Bridewell, the clerk of Westminster gatehouse and two others. Austin, as it was his usual custom, examined the irons and hand cuffs and found all safe and firm, and then left me; and he may remember that I asked him to come again to me the same evening, but I neither expected or desired his company; and happy was it for the poor man that he did not interfere while I had the large iron bar in my hand, though I once had a design to have barricaded him or any others from coming into the room while I was at work, but then considering that such a project would be useless, I let fall that resolution.

As near as I can remember, just before three in the afternoon I went to work, taking off first my handcuffs; next with main strength I twisted a small iron link of the chain between my legs asunder, and the broken pieces proved extreme useful to me in my design. The fetlocks I drew up to the calves of my legs, taking off before that my stockings, and with my garters made them firm to my body to prevent them shackling. I then proceeded to make a hole in the chimney of the Castle about three foot wide and six foot high from the floor, and with the help of the broken links aforesaid wrenched an iron bar out of the chimney, of about two feet and an half in length and an inch square: a most notable implement. I immediately entered the Red Room directly over the Castle, where some of the Preston rebels had been kept a long time agone; and as the keepers say, the door had not been unlocked for seven years; but I intended not to be seven years in opening it. I went to work upon the nut of the lock and with little difficulty got it off and made the door fly before me. In this room I found a large nail which proved of great use in my farther progress. The door of the entry between the Red Room and the chapel proved an hard task, it being a laborious piece of work; for here I was forced to break away the wall and dislodge the bolt which was fastened on the other side. This occasioned much noise, and I was very fearful of being heard by the Master Side debtors. Being got to the chapel, I climbed over the iron spikes and with ease broke one of them off for my further purposes, and opened the door on the inside. The door going out of the chapel to the leads, I stripped the nut from off the lock, as I had done before from that of the Red Room, and then got into the entry between the chapel and the leads and came to another strong door, which being fastened by a very strong lock, there I had like to have stopped, and it being full dark, my spirits began to fail me, as greatly doubting of succeeding; but cheering up, I wrought on with great diligence, and in less than half an hour, with the main help of the nail from the Red Room and the spike from the chapel, wrenched the box off and so made the door my humble servant.

A little further in my passage, another stout door stood in my way, and this was guarded with more bolts, bars and locks than any I had hitherto met with. I had by this time great encouragement, as hoping soon to be rewarded for all this toil and labour. The clock at St Sepulchre's was now going the eighth hour, and this proved a very useful hint to me soon after. I went first upon the box and the nut, but found it labour in vain; and then proceeded to attack the fillet of the door. This succeeded beyond expectation, for the box of the lock came off with it from the main post. I found my work was near finished and that my fate soon would be determined.

I was got to a door opening in the lower leads, which being only bolted on the inside, I opened it with ease and then clambered from the top of it to the higher leads and went over the wall. I saw the streets were lighted, the shops being still open, and therefore began to consider what was necessary to be further done, as knowing that the smallest accident would still spoil the whole workmanship, and was doubtful on which of the houses I should alight. I found I must go back for the blanket which had been my covering anights in the Castle, which I accordingly did, and endeavoured to fasten my stockings and that together, to lessen my descent, but wanted necessaries so to do and was therefore forced to make use of the blanket alone. I fixed the same with the chapel spike into the wall of Newgate and dropped from it on the turner's leads, a house adjoining to the prison.

'Twas then about nine of the clock and the shops not yet shut in. It fortunately happened that the garret door on the leads was open. I stole softly down about two pair of stairs and then heard company talking in a room, the door open. My irons gave a small clink, which made a woman cry, 'Lord, what noise is that?' A man replied, 'Perhaps the dog or cat.' And so it went off. I returned up to the garret and laid myself down, being terribly fatigued, and continued there for about two hours and then crept down once more to the room where the company were and heard a gentleman taking his leave, being very importunate to be gone, saying he had disappointed friends by not going home sooner. In about three quarters more, the gentleman took leave and went, being lighted down stairs by the maid, who, when she returned, shut the chamber door. I resolved at all hazards to follow, and slipped downstairs, but made a stumble against a chamber door. I was instantly in the entry and out at the street door, which I was so unmannerly as not to shut after me. I was once more, contrary to my own expectation and that of all mankind, a free man.

I passed directly by St Sepulchre's watch-house, bidding them good morrow, it being after twelve, and down Snow Hill, up Holborn, leaving St Andrew's watch on my left, and then again passed the watch-house at Holborn Bar and made down Gray's Inn Lane into the Fields, and at two in the morning came to Tottenham Court and there got into an old house in the fields where cows had sometime been kept, and laid me down to rest and slept well for three hours. My legs were swelled and bruised intolerably, which gave me great uneasiness; and, having my fetters still on, I dreaded the approach of the day, fearing

69

then I should be discovered. I began to examine my pockets and found myself master of between forty and fifty shillings. I had no friend in the world that I could send to or trust with my condition. About seven on Friday morning, it began raining and continued so the whole day, insomuch that not one creature was to be seen in the fields. I would freely have parted with my right hand for a hammer, a chisel and a punch. I kept snug in my retreat till the evening, when after dark I ventured into Tottenham and got to a little blind chandler's shop and there furnished myself with cheese and bread, small beer and other necessaries, hiding my irons with a great coat as much as possible. I asked the woman for a hammer, but there was none to be had, so I went back very quietly to my dormitory and rested pretty well that night and continued there all Saturday. At night, I went again to the chandler's shop and got provisions and slept till about six the next day, which being Sunday, I began with a stone to batter the basils of the fetters in order to beat them into a large oval and then to slip my heels through.

In the afternoon, the master of the shed or house came in and, seeing my irons, asked me, 'For God's sake, who are you?' I told him 'an unfortunate young man who had been sent to Bridewell about a bastard child, as not being able to give security to the parish, and had made my escape'. The man replied, if that was the case it was a small fault indeed, for he had been guilty of the same things himself formerly; and withal said, however, he did not like my looks, and cared not how soon I was gone.

After he was gone, observing a poor-looking man like a joiner, I made up to him and repeated the same story, assuring him that twenty shillings should be at his service if he could furnish me with a smith's hammer and a punch. The man proved a shoemaker by trade, but willing to obtain the reward immediately borrowed the tools of a blacksmith his neighbour and likewise gave me great assistance, and before five that evening I had entirely got rid of those troublesome companions my fetters, which I gave to the fellow, besides his twenty shillings, if he thought fit to make use of them.

That night, I came to a cellar at Charing Cross and refreshed very comfortably with roast veal, etc., where about a dozen people were all discoursing about Sheppard, and nothing else was talked on whilst I stayed amongst them. I had tied an handkerchief about my head, tore my woollen cap in many places, as likewise my coat and stockings, and looked exactly like what I designed to represent, a beggar fellow.

The next day, I took shelter at an alehouse of little or no trade in Rupert Street, near Piccadilly. The woman and I discoursed much about Sheppard. I assured her it was impossible for him to escape out of the kingdom, and that the keepers would have him again in a few days. The woman wished that a curse might fall on those who should betray him. I continued there till the evening, when I stepped towards the Haymarket and mixed with a crowd about two ballad-singers, the subject being about Sheppard. And I remember the company was very merry about the matter.

On Tuesday, I hired a garret for my lodging at a poor house in Newport Market, and sent for a sober young woman who for a long time had been the real mistress of my affections, who came to me and rendered all the assistance she was capable of affording. I made her the messenger to my mother, who lodged in Clare Street. She likewise visited me in a day or two after, begging on her bended knees of me to make the best of my way out of the kingdom, which I faithfully promised; but I cannot say it was in my intentions heartily to do so.

I was oftentimes in Spitalfields, Drury Lane, Lewkenor's Lane, Parker's Lane, St Thomas Street, etc., those having been the chief scenes of my rambles and pleasures.

I had once formed a design to have opened a shop or two in Monmouth Street for some necessaries, but let that drop and came to a resolution of breaking the house of the two Mr Rawlins brothers, pawnbrokers in Drury Lane, which accordingly I put in execution and succeeded, they both hearing me rifling their goods as they lay in bed together in the next room. And though there were none others to assist me, I pretended there was, by loudly giving out directions for shooting the first person through the head that presumed to stir: which effectually quieted them while I carried off my booty – with part whereof on the fatal Saturday following, being the 31st of October, I made an extraordinary appearance and from a carpenter and butcher was now transformed into a perfect gentleman; and in company with my sweetheart aforesaid and another young woman her acquaintance went into the City and were very merry together at a public house not far from the place of my old confinement. At four that same afternoon, we all passed under Newgate in a hackney coach, the windows drawn up, and in the evening I sent for my mother to the Shears alehouse in Maypole Alley near Claremarket, and with her drank three quarterns of brandy; and after leaving her I drank in one place or other about the neighbourhood all evening, till the evil hour of twelve, having been seen and known by many of my acquaintance, all of them cautioning me and wondering at my presumption to appear in that manner. At length, my senses were quite overcome with the quantities and variety of liquors I had all the day been drinking of, which paved the way for my fate to meet me. When apprehended, I do protest, I was altogether incapable of resisting and scarce knew what they were doing to me, and had but two second-hand pistols scarce worth carrying about me.

Having already been convicted, he was brought before Mr Justice Powis in the Court of King's Bench, Westminster Hall, on 10 November. He was offered the chance of having his sentence reduced by informing on his associates, but unlike his brother and many others before him he refused to take such a way out. Sentence of death was passed on him, and a rule of court was made for his execution on the following Monday. He regularly attended prayers in the chapel, but though he behaved with some dignity, he entered apparently finding everything a great joke and did what he could to prevent any degree of seriousness among the other prisoners on their return. Yet when he came up to chapel, he suddenly appeared very serious, listening and assisting with great attention at Divine Service, though upon other occasions he avoided any religious discourse as much as he could. Several prominent people sent a petition to King George I, begging for his sentence of death to be commuted to transportation. To the Revd Wagstaffe who visited him, he said, according to Defoe, 'One file's worth all the Bibles in the World'.

Even on the day of his execution he had apparently not given up all hope of eluding justice, and hoped to cheat his fate a final time. Having a penknife in his pocket, he hoped to use it to cut the cord that bound his arms, so he could throw himself out of the cart among the crowd, and run through the narrow passage where the sheriff's officers on horseback would find it impossible to follow him. There was every chance, he reckoned, that some of the more sympathetic spectators would help him to get back among the crowd, into Lincoln's Inn Fields, and then to the Thames. This scheme might have had a fair chance of success, had it not been for the fact that before he left the press-yard Mr Watson, a prison warder, searched his pockets, and found the knife, cutting himself badly in the process.

Yet Sheppard was the eternal optimist. Believing he could still be preserved after execution, he asked his friends if they could put him into a warm bed as soon as he had been cut down, and try to open a vein, which he had been told would restore him to life. By now he and his adventures had become the main topic of conversation about town. Numbers flocked daily to behold him, and far from being displeased at being made a spectacle of, he talked lightheartedly of his escapades to all who would listen.

The crowds at Newgate included men and women from all ranks of life, including gentry and peers. The noise made about him, it was said, 'and this curiosity of persons of so high a rank, was a very great misfortune to the poor wretch himself, who from these circumstances began to conceive grand ideas of himself, as well as strong hopes of pardon, which encouraged him to play over all his airs and divert as many as thought it worth their while by their presence to prevent a dying man from considering his latter end, who instead of repenting of his crimes, gloried in rehearsing them'.

While being taken in a cart to his execution at Tyburn on 16 November 1724, suitably handcuffed, he behaved with dignity. As the cart was drawn along Holborn and Oxford Street to the gallows, accompanied by a mounted City Marshal and liveried Javelin Men, there was something of a carnival air in the streets, a warm-hearted farewell which hardly seemed appropriate for a man about to go to his death. Instead the people of London had taken the opportunity to stage a celebration of Sheppard's life. The procession halted at the City of Oxford tavern on Oxford Street, where he drank a pint of sack. The cheerful atmosphere continued at Tyburn, and copies of his 'official' autobiography, ghostwritten by Daniel Defoe, were on sale. Sheppard handed a sheet paper to someone as he mounted the scaffold, perhaps as a symbolic endorsement of the account in the Narrative.

After mounting the gallows, he confessed to having committed two robberies, of Mr Philips and Mrs Cook, for which he had been tried and acquitted. Yet he still denied that he and Joseph Blake had William Field in their company when they broke open the house of Mr Kneebone.

His slight build had been an advantage while escaping, but on the day of reckoning it condemned him to a slow death by strangulation in the hangman's noose. After being suspended for the allotted fifteen minutes, his body was cut down. The crowd feared that his body would be taken away instantly for dissection, and they pressed forward to prevent anyone from doing such a thing. They thus inadvertently prevented his friends from implementing the plan to take his body to a doctor in an attempt to revive him. When he was cut down his body was delivered to his friends, who carried him to a public-house in Long Acre, and then to burial in the churchyard of St Martin's-in-the-Field. Over 200,000 people, about one-third of the total population of London, were estimated to have witnessed the scene, and a riot which broke out concerning the disposal of his corpse was quelled by soldiers with fixed bayonets.

On the following Sunday following parishioners heard a sermon on the occasion of Sheppard's escape:

Now, my beloved, what a melancholy consideration it is, that men should shew so much regard for the preservation of a poor perishing body, that can remain at most but for a few years; and at the same time be so unaccountably negligent of a precious soul, which must continue to the age of eternity! Oh, what care! what pains! what diligence! and what contrivances are made use of for, and laid out upon, these frail and tottering tabernacles of clay: when, alas! the nobler part of us is allowed so very small a share of our concern that we scarce will give ourselves the trouble of bestowing a thought upon it.

We have a remarkable instance of this in a notorious malefactor, well known by the name of Jack Sheppard! What amazing difficulties has he overcome, what astonishing things has he performed, for the sake of a stinking, miserable carcass, hardly worth hanging? how dexterously did he pick the padlock of his chain with a crooked nail? How manfully did he burst his fetters asunder, climb up the chimney, wrench out an iron bar, break his way through a stone wall and make the strong doors of a dark entry fly before him, till he got upon the leads of the prison? and then, fixing a blanket to the wall with a spike he stole out of the chapel, how intrepidly did he descend to the top of the turner's house, and how cautiously pass down the stairs and make his escape at the street door?

Oh, that ye were all like Jack Sheppard! - Mistake me not, my brethren, I don't mean in a carnal but in a spiritual sense, for I mean to spiritualize these things.- What a shame it would be if we should not think it worth our while to take as much pains and employ as many deep thoughts to save our souls, as he has done to preserve his body.

Let me exhort ye, then, to open the locks of your hearts with the nail of repentance; burst asunder the fetters of your beloved lusts; mount the chimney of hope, take from hence the bar of good resolution, break through the stone wall of despair and all the strong holds in the dark entry of the valley of the shadow of death; raise yourself to the leads of divine meditation; fix the blanket of faith with the spike of the church; let yourselves down to the turner's house of resignation and descend the stairs of humility. So shall you come to the door of deliverance from the prison of iniquity and escape the clutches of that old executioner and devil, who goeth about like a roaring lion, seeking whom he may devour.

The notice for Sheppard's arrest after his escape from the Castle described him as 'about 22 years old, about five foot four inches high, very slender, of a pale complexion, has an impediment or hesitation in his speech'. His robberies, it was said, were characterised by adroitness and skill rather than violence, and his courage, his loyalty to companions, and his cheery if impudent disposition lend some colour to popular portrayals of him as a likeable rogue. On the other hand, it could hardly be said of him that his crimes were prompted by necessity, and he became a persistent and – as the Kneebone robbery demonstrated - undiscriminating thief.

Sheppard's case coincided with the bringing to justice of another of Wild's more notorious associates, Joseph Blake, a highwayman and Sheppard's partner-in-crime. Blake was born in 1700, his parents Nathaniel and Jane being described as having been 'in tolerable Circumstances', and had a sister, Jane. He attended St Giles Cripplegate parish school for about six years, distinguished only by an early 'Inclination to Roguery'. At about fourteen he was introduced by his school fellow and future companion in crime William Blewitt, who was hanged for murder in 1726. Soon after this fateful meeting Blake left school and embarked on a career of robbery. It was also thought that from childhood or at any rate adolescence, he had been under Wild's tuition, who paid for the curing of his wounds, allowed him 3s 6d a week for his subsistence while he was in the Compter, and afforded his help to get him out of there at last.

According to one account, by the age of fifteen he had been in all the Bridewells, and Workhouses about Town. He began his criminal career in earnest at about seventeen, picking pockets in Company with Edward Pollit whom he was said to have later impeached in order to save his own life. A thoroughly inept thief, he spent much of his life trying to avoid Bridewell, and usually failing. By 1719 he had acquired a nickname, 'Blueskin', thought to have been on account of his dark complexion or facial hair, or as a pun on William Blewitt's surname. He also went thieving as part of a gang led by the Irish highwayman James Carrick. In 1722 he joined a group of street robbers led by Robert Wilkinson, and while out with them one night they robbed Mr Clark of eight shillings and a silver hilted sword. A woman who was looking out of her window saw them and raised the alarm. Wilkinson fired a pistol at her, but she moved her head and the bullet merely grazed the window.

Blake was with the same gang when they attacked Captain Langley at the corner of Hyde Park Road as he was going to the camp, but failed to steal anything from him. Soon afterwards Wilkinson was apprehended, and informed against several others, among them Blake and Lock. The latter produced evidence before Justice Blackerby, with details of no less than seventy robberies, upon which he was also admitted a witness. In addition he named Wilkinson, Lincoln, Carrick and Carroll, and himself, as the five murderers of Peter Martain, a Chelsea pensioner, by the Park wall. Wilkinson was apprehended, and despite informing on the others he was tried and convicted. Blake also gave evidence against the rest of his companions, and discovered about a dozen robberies which they had committed, including one in which two gentlemen in hunting-caps were together in a chariot on the Hampstead Road, from whom they took two gold watches, rings, seals and other things to a considerable value. Levey laid his pistol down by the gentlemen all the while he searched them, yet they wanted either the courage or the presence of mind to seize it and prevent their losing things of so great value.

At a time when violent crime and the 'Insolency' of highwaymen and footpads in and around the metropolis seemed to be reaching epidemic proportions, there was scarcely a robbery in or near London in which Blake was not involved. In the summer of 1722 several of his associates were apprehended, and three were hanged in September. Blake, who was probably screened from justice by Wild, was lucky to escape from justice for a time, and when he was arrested in December 1722 he was admitted as an evidence against several of his companions, including his old friend William Blewitt. Soon after this Oakey, Levey and Blake stopped a man in Fig Lane. He did not surrender as easily as they expected, so Levey and Oakey beat him over the head with their pistols, leaving him badly wounded, and taking one guinea from his pocket. In February 1723 after Blake gave evidence against them, Levey, Oakey and Flood were executed for robbing Colonel Cope and Mr Young of the watch. Carrick and Malony had already been executed.

After having helped the guardians of law and order to hang so many of his associates, Blake thought himself entitled to a free pardon and a reward. His hopes were not to be realised, as he had not surrendered willingly and quietly; on the contrary, he had only been captured after putting up a spirited show of resistance. He remained a prisoner in the Wood Street Compter, subsisting on the charity of Wild, obstinately refusing to be transported for seven years, till at last prevailing with two Gardeners to stand surety for his good behaviour, he was carried before a worthy alderman of the City and released in the spring of 1724. One man present asking how long might be given him before they should see him again at the Old Bailey, one man answered, 'In about three sessions'. It proved an accurate prediction, as three sessions later Blake was indeed brought to the bar.

No sooner was Blake at liberty than he went back to his thieving ways, and joined with Jack Sheppard to search for prey in the fields. During the summer of 1724 the pair committed several robberies on Hampstead Heath. Near the halfway house to Hampstead they met a man who was extremely drunk. Blake immediately knocked him down into the ditch, where he would have perished had not Sheppard took pity on him and kept his head above the mud, albeit with some difficulty. At the next sessions, two brothers named Brightwell in the Guards Regiment were tried for the crime. Had it not been for several men who could vouch for their having been on duty at the time the robbery was committed they would probably have been convicted on the highly suspect prosecutor's evidence. The elder Brightwell died a week after being released from custody, and did not live to see his innocence fully cleared by the confession of Blake.

The latter found sureties for his good behaviour, and was released in June 1724. He then joined Jack Sheppard* to burgle the house of William Kneebone (Sheppard's former apprentice master) on 12 July, stealing a quantity of cloth and some other trinkets, stored them near the horse ferry at Westminster, and rather unwisely approached one of Wild's fences, William Field, to sell them. It was well known that Field was in the pay of Wild, and whether because Blake's exploits had 'made such a noise about Town, that Wild did not think it safe to countenance him any longer', or because Wild objected to Blake's association with Sheppard who it was believed,obstinately refused to have any dealings with the 'Thief-Catcher', it became apparent that the latter was going to turn his protégé in.

On 3 October 1724 Blake was apprehended in his St Giles lodgings by Wild and Arnold and was held in Newgate, charged with Sheppard on Field's evidence with the Kneebone robbery. Field claimed that he had taken part in this burglary but was turning King's evidence, a claim which both Blake and Sheppard would vehemently deny at their respective trials. About then days later Blake was outside the Old Bailey court house waiting to be arraigned, and to pass the time shared a glass of wine and conversation with his old master. He took the opportunity to plead with Wild in the courtroom to have his sentence commuted from hanging to transportation, since he had worked for him before. Blake was sure this would prove no problem, but Wild refused to help. The only dubious comfort he could offer the soon-to-be-sentenced Blake was that his body should be handsomely interred in a good coffin at his own expense. It would be vanity for him to flatter himself with hopes for any more than that, and he had better prepare himself for another life. Wild was prepared to make him a gift of money to support him during his remaining in Newgate, and any books he might want - but there was no hope of getting him transported.

Blake, who had expected that the master thief-taker would grant his every wish, was enraged. He took a clasp-knife from his pocket, seized Wild and clapped a hand under his chin, then slit his throat from the ear to beyond the windpipe. Everyone present was aghast, fearing that the wound could easily prove fatal. Had this been the case, he would have been spared the eventual fate which would consign him to oblivion within a few months. Covered with blood, he collapsed and was taken to a surgeon for treatment. Blake was probably not the only one who had harboured dreams of putting Wild to death. Many of the other villains with whom he had worked, those who had not been sent to the gallows, had doubtless nursed similar thoughts at one time or another.

Wild soon recovered from the attack, but his injuries prevented him from testifying at Blake's trial three days later. After putting up a half-hearted defence, aimed

*See p. 43

primarily at discrediting Field's evidence, Blake was found guilty of burglary and sentenced to death. Blake's attempt on Wild's life, immortalized in the street ballad Newgate's Garland, elevated him to something of the status of a popular hero. 'Amongst the Mob' he was viewed as a 'brave Fellow', and by numerous respectable citizens as one of the many unfortunate 'foster children' whom Wild had 'bred up in the Art of Thieving' only to deliver to the gallows. Sheppard himself was supposed to have characterised the man whom later literature would cast as his staunch sidekick as 'a worthless Companion' and 'a sorry Thief'.

Blake showed no remorse for what he had done. He declared that if he had thought of it before, he would have armed himself with an even sharper knife suitable for cutting off Wild's head and throwing it amongst the rabble in Sessions House Yard, where it richly deserved to be. At the time of his sentence there was a woman with him also about to be condemned for a similar offence. They were both placed in the Bail Dock at the Old Bailey, and Blake was so rude to her that she burst into sobs and wept aloud, to the consternation of everyone on the Bench.

While described by witnesses as being duly serious, penitent and even tearful at chapel, Blake did not seem in the least penitent for his actions in the days leading up to his execution, except for the failure of his attempt on Wild, and busied himself with various abortive escape attempts. All the time he lay under condemnation, he appeared 'utterly thoughtless and insensible of his approaching fate. Though from the cutting of Wild's throat and some other barbarities of the same nature he acquired amongst the mob the character of a brave fellow, yet he was said to be in himself but a mean spirited, feeble man, and never exerted himself but through either fury or despair. Some acknowledged that he was 'a Dapper, well-set Fellow, of great Strength', but dismissed him 'as a mean spirited timorous Wretch', who ruthlessly betrayed most of his associates, and a brute who, upon being locked up after his trial, violently - and in full view of the court - attempted 'Rudeness' with 'a Woman Prisoner'. He wept much at the chapel before he was to die; and though he drank much to try and dull his sorrows, 'yet at the place of execution he wept again, trembled, and showed all the signs of a timorous confusion as well he might, who had, lived wickedly, and trifled with his repentance to the grave'. He was remembered as a smartly-dressed if hardly handsome man, 'possessed of great strength and great cruelty; equally detested by the sober part of the world for the audacious wickedness of his behaviour, and despised by his companions for the villainies he committed even against them'. Even on his way to Tyburn, Blake tried with the tacit consent of spectators 'to escape out of the Cart', and after this project was prevented stopped at the Griffin tavern in Holborn, 'where he drank and shewed much Insolence and ill Behaviour'. By all accounts, when he mounted the scaffold on 11 November 1724 he was so 'disguised in Liquor' as to 'reel and Faulter in his Speech'.

Another thief with whom Wild had worked survived him by two or three years, though he met a similar fate. Edward Bellamy had at one time been a tailor's apprentice, but close liaison with some extravagant prostitutes led him to resort to more dubious ways of making money. He fell in with a crowd of pickpockets, and they would go in groups of three or four to silversmiths' shops. Their ploy was for one of them to pretend to try and steal something of little value, thus distracting the shopkeeper while another would make off with something considerably better. From this, they progressed to walking the streets at night, trying to force shop windows with a chisel and then run off with any property within their reach. Later he turned to forgery, which was not then a capital offence, and through passing a forged note defrauded a draper of a large amount. He was apprehended and lodged in Newgate, but his friends found means to accommodate the matter with the injured party and he was discharged without being brought to trial.

Soon after this he met Wild, whose achievements he no doubt longed to emulate. Wild was then in the habit of borrowing large sums from Mr Wildgoose, a Smithfield innkeeper. Bellamy asked Wild to recommend him to Wildgoose as a possible partner, but Wild refused. As he had often gone with messages and notes from Wild to Wildgoose, and being familiar with Wild's handwriting, he forged a draft on the latter for ten guineas, which Wildgoose paid without hesitation. Once Bellamy had the money he ceased paying his usual visits at Wild's office. A few days later Wild went to his acquaintance to borrow some money, when Wildgoose told him he had paid his draft for the sum already. When he had produced the note, Wild could not be sure that it was not his own handwriting, other than by recalling that he had never given such a draft. Wildgoose was not familiar with Bellamy's name; but when he gave a description of his person, Wild soon found who had committed the forgery, and ordered his minions to be careful to apprehend the offender.

Once Bellamy was found in a lodging in Whitefriars, Wild's men advised their master that they had him in custody, and asked for orders on how they should dispose of him. Meanwhile Bellamy, who expected no mercy from Wild, seized the advantage of the casual absence of his attendants from the room, fixed a rope to the bar of the window, and let himself into the street, though the room was three storeys high. He thought of accommodating the affair with Wild, as he imagined he would be treated with the utmost severity if he should be reapprehended; but before he could do so Wild's men seized him at a gin-shop in Chancery Lane, and again sent to their master for further instructions. Wild told them that they might allow him his freedom as long as he came to the office and 'adjusted the business with himself'. Bellamy was thus discharged, but as he knew it would be dangerous to antagonise Wild, he went next morning to an inn in the Old Bailey, where he sent for Wild to breakfast with him. The latter sent for Wildgoose, Bellamy gave him a note for the money received, and the affair was regarded as closed.

Bellamy soon returned to his old thieving ways, and committed a large number of robberies in the City of London. He and one of his gang having broken the sash of a silversmith's shop in Russell Court, Drury Lane, a person who lay under the counter fired a blunderbuss at them, which obliged them to leave without taking their booty. Frustrated by their failure, they went to the house of another silversmith, which they broke open, and finding the servant-maid sitting up for her master, they terrified her into silence, and carried off effects to some considerable value. Not long after this robbery, they broke open the shop of a grocer near Shoreditch, in the expectation at finding cash to a great amount; but the proprietor having previously secured it, they got only about ten pounds of tea, and the loose money in the tin. Their next attempt was at the house of a hosier in Widegate Alley, from whose shop they carried off some goods of value, which they sold on the following day. From the shop of a silversmith in Bride-lane, they took plate worth £50; and from the house of a haberdasher in Bishopsgate Street, various items, then proceeded to dispose of the lot.

On another occasion they broke open a tea shop near Gray's Inn Lane, by cutting away part of the shutters with chisels. They were going to lift up the sash, when a person from inside heard them, cried out 'thieves!' and they ran off empty-handed. Having broken into a tea-warehouse near Aldgate, they had packed up a valuable parcel of goods, when the maid servant came downstairs without a candle. She went into the yard, and came back indoors unaware that they were in the house, but when she saw them Bellamy seized her and made her lie on the floor, while they went off with their booty. That same night they broke open the shop of a mercer in Bishopsgate Street, carrying off another large quantity of goods. Their next robbery was at the house of a grocer in Thames Street. The watchman passed by as they were packing up their booty, Bellamy seized him and obliged him to put out his candle, to prevent any alarm being given. Having kept him till they were ready to go off with their plunder, they took him to the side of the Thames, and threatened to throw him in, if he would not throw in his lantern and staff. The poor man had no choice but to comply. Soon after this they stole a large sum of money and various goods from the house of a grocer which they broke open in Aldersgate Street. A neighbour saw them from his window, but was too frightened to report it to the authorities.

Next they plundered at an old clothes-shop, kept by a woman in Shadwell, and removed everything of value, followed by the shop of a hosier in Coleman Street, taking away goods worth £70, which they shared out and sold. After this they went to break open the house of a linen-draper in Westminster, but they were surprised in the act and had to leave empty-handed. On the following evening, as they noticed the door of a shop shut in St Clement's churchyard, they tied it firmly with a cord on the outside. Throwing up the sash, they stole a large number of silk handkerchiefs, while the woman in the shop tried in vain several times to open the door. That same night they stole a variety of plate, clothes, and other property from two houses in Holborn.

At around the same time they were working hand in glove with an elderly woman who had opened an office near Leicester Fields for the reception of stolen goods, similar to Wild's enterprises. Bellamy and his companions regularly sold her many of their ill-gotten gains. On one occasion she gave them rather less money than they expected and Bellamy, intent on revenge, went to her office with a small quantity of stolen plate. While she was out, showing it to a silversmith, he stole a large sum of cash from her premises, and then robbed a shop in Monmouth Street. By this time he had become such a public enemy that a reward of £100 was offered for his capture. He was arrested on the following day, committed to Newgate, tried, convicted, and sentenced. From then until the arrival of the warrant for his execution, he swore that he would be hanged in his shroud. Just before his execution at Tyburn on 27 March 1728, he faced the crowds to confess his offences, and admit that he knew his sentence was fair.

Aldgate

CHAPTER EIGHT

Wild's Decline and Fall

Public opinion was now turning firmly against Wild as a result of his involvement in the arrest and prosecution of Sheppard and Blake. The press had championed Sheppard's cause as an underdog hero who had resisted having any dealings with Wild, and using him as a mouthpiece to denounce the highly dubious, if not shameless, practice of thief-catching, as well as Blake as an example of one of the many 'foster children' whom Wild had trained as a thief and later brought to the gallows. The man who had long been the celebrated thief-taker and master policeman of London was now becoming the personification of brutal, unjust authority, and it would not take much to bring his empire tumbling down around him.

About a year or two earlier Wild had purchased a sloop to transport goods to Holland and Flanders, and as his captain appointed Roger Johnson, who had had a notorious reputation as a thief though he had somehow eluded being caught. The vessel normally sailed for Ostend, but sometimes took goods to other ports such as Bruges, Ghent and Brussels. Wild also used it to bring home large shipments of lace, wine, and brandy, ensuring that these commodities were landed under cover of darkness, in order to evade the payment of duty to the revenue officers. On one journey five pieces of lace were lost, and Johnson deducted the value of them from the mate's pay. The furious mate informed on Johnson to the revenue officers, and the vessel was exchequered, which meant an indefinite delay in obtaining the release of the ship. Even if the case failed, and the ship was returned to the defendants, they would be unable to make any claim for damages or costs. Johnson was ordered to pay back damages of £700 and the commercial proceedings were entirely ruined. In disgust, he returned to his old life of thieving.

There had long been bad blood between Johnson and another thief, Thomas Edwards, who presided over a robbers' haven in Long Lane, regarding the division of some booty. When they met in the Strand one day they turned each other in, and were both taken into custody. Wild stood bail for Johnson, but Edwards was not prosecuted. When he was set free again he informed against Wild, and when the latter's private warehouses were searched, a vast amount of stolen goods was found. Wild now arrested Edwards in the name of Johnson, to whom he pretended the goods belonged, and Edwards was taken to the Marshalsea, but within a day he was released on bail. Edwards was determined to get even with Johnson, and did his best to find him. At length he met him accidentally in Whitechapel Road, and gave him into the custody of a peace-officer, who took him to a nearby inn pending putting him in custody. Johnson sent for Wild, who immediately appeared, accompanied by the ever-faithful Quilt Arnold. Wild created a diversion by inciting a riot, which Johnson used to advantage by making a swift getaway.

The constables were now looking for Wild in order to help him apprehend Johnson, and Wild, suspecting his best days were behind him, decided it would be prudent to lie low for a while. He temporarily ceased his activities and made himself scarce, but Mr Jones, a constable of the Holborn division, had been warned to keep an eye out for him. He went to Wild's house in the Old Bailey on 15 February 1725, apprehended him and Arnold, and took them before Sir John Fryer, who committed them to Newgate on a charge of having assisted in Johnson's escape. What had become of Johnson is unknown.

The trial and execution of Blake had openly raised serious doubts about Wild's scruples, or lack of them. He had long since been so notorious that it would now take little for the authorities to find something with which to charge him. On Wednesday 24 February, Wild moved to be either admitted to bail or discharged, or brought to trial at the sessions. On the following Friday a warrant of detainer was produced in Court, listing the charges being brought against him.

I.   That for many years he had been a confederate with great numbers of highwaymen, pickpockets, housebreakers, shoplifters, and other thieves.

II.   That he had formed a kind of corporation of thieves, of which he was the head or director; and that notwithstanding his pretended services, in detecting and prosecuting offenders, he procured such only to be hanged as concealed their booty, or refused to share it with him.

III.   That he had divided the town and country into so many districts, and appointed distinct gangs for each, who regularly accounted with him for their robberies. That he had also a particular set to steal at churches in time of divine service: and likewise other moving detachments to attend at Court on birthdays, balls, &c, and at both houses of parliament, circuits, and country fairs.

IV.   That the persons employed by him were for the most part felon convicts, who had returned from transportation before the time for which they were transported was expired; and that he made choice of them to be his agents, because they could not be legal evidences against him, and because he had it in his power to take from them what part of the stolen goods he thought fit, and otherwise use them ill, or hang them, as he pleased.

V. That he had from time to time supplied such convicted felons with money and clothes, and lodged them in his own house, the better to conceal them: particularly some against whom there are now informations for counterfeiting and diminishing broad pieces and guineas.

VI. That he had not only been a receiver of stolen goods, as well as of writings of all kinds, for near fifteen years past, but had frequently been a confederate, and robbed along with the above-mentioned convicted felons.

VII. That in order to carry on these vile practices, and to gain some credit with the ignorant multitude, he usually carried a short silver staff, as a badge of authority from the government, which he used to produce when he himself was concerned in robbing.

VIII. That he had, under his care and direction, several warehouses for receiving and concealing stolen goods; and also a ship for carrying off jewels, watches, and other valuable goods, to Holland, where he had a superannuated thief for his factor.

IX. That he kept in pay several artists to make alterations, and transform watches, seals, snuff-boxes, rings, and other valuable things, that they might not be known, several of which he used to present to such persons as he thought might be of service to him.

X. That he seldom or never helped the owners to the notes and papers they had lost unless he found them able exactly to specify and describe them, and then often insisted on more than half the value.

XI. And, lastly, it appears that he has often sold human blood, by procuring false evidence to swear persons into facts they were not guilty of; sometimes to prevent them from being evidences against himself, and at other times for the sake of the great reward given by the government.

An affidavit from Mr Jones was also read in Court, stating that two persons would be produced to accuse the prisoner of capital offences. The men alluded to were John Follard and Thomas Butler, both convicted of robbery. However it was considered expedient to grant them a pardon on condition of their appearing in support of a prosecution against Wild. They had pleaded guilty to the same offences, and were remanded to Newgate till the next sessions. There was still no exact charge against Wild, and it seems that the authorities were still casting about for prosecution witnesses when on 10 March Wild obligingly saved them that trouble by committing a felony while in Newgate. He was careless enough to accept ten guineas for returning some stolen lace to a Mrs Statham, without making any attempt to prosecute the thieves who had committed the robbery on his instructions.

On 12 April Wild's counsel asked that his trial might be postponed till the next sessions. An affidavit made by the prisoner was read in Court, asserting that until the previous evening he was entirely ignorant of a bill having been found against him, that he had no knowledge of what offence he was being charged with, and that he was unable to procure two vital witnesses, one living near Brentford, and the other in Somerset. This was opposed by the counsel for the crown, who urged that it would be improper to defer the trial on so frivolous a pretext as that made by the prisoner.

It was foolish of him, they said, to apply for an affidavit expressing ignorance of the offence with which he was charged, while at the same time he declared that two nameless persons were material witnesses.

The trial occurred at the same time as that of Thomas Parker, 1st Earl of Macclesfield, for taking £100,000 in bribes and embezzling public money. The Earl had briefly been Regent of Great Britain in 1714 on the death of Queen Anne until her successor George, Elector of Hanover, could arrive in England to take up the crown as King George I. Two years later the politician had been appointed Lord Chancellor, though he resigned his office in 1724. He was impeached, struck off the roll of the Privy Council, fined £30,000 and imprisoned in the Tower of London until payment was made. Corruption in high and low places was rife, and the public was only too glad to see such public figures receive their come-uppance.

Wild's arrest came as no surprise, and many thought it was long overdue. During his imprisonment, articles in the press were complaining that for many years now it had seemed as if nobody could be acquitted, condemned, reprieved or hanged, except at the pleasure of 'honest Jonathan'. It was further disclosed that far from combating the crime wave, Wild had been the main instigator behind so many organised felonies. He had made no more than token attempts to suppress the criminal underworld, and was in fact the evil genius at whose door much of it could be laid. His 'Lost Property office' was nothing more than a clearing house for large quantities of stolen merchandise supplied to him by his gangs. There was barely a misdemeanour in which he had not had a significant hand, be it forgery, coining, smuggling, or protection rackets on brothels and gaming houses.

Now members of Wild's gang realised that their leader had been well and truly caught, they began to come forward, producing evidence against him. In little time all his activities, including his grand scheme of running and then hanging thieves, became public knowledge. At the same time, evidence came to light concerning his frequent bribery of public officers.

Wild informed the Court that his witnesses were Hays, at the Pack Horse, Turnham Green, and Wilson, a clothier at Frome. He had also heard it said that he was indicted for a felony upon a Mrs Stretham. His counsel moved that the names of Hays and Wilson might be inserted in the affidavit, and that it should be again sworn to by their client. The counsel for the prosecution observed that justice would not be denied the prisoner, though he could not expect any extraordinary favours or indulgences. Follard and Butler were bound each in the penalty of £500 to appear at the ensuing sessions, when it was agreed that Wild's fate should be determined.

On 15 May 1725 Jonathan Wild was indicted for stealing fifty yards of lace from the house of Catherine Stretham, in the parish of St Andrew, Holborn, on 22 January. A second indictment was issued against him for feloniously receiving from her, on 10 March, ten guineas, on account, and under pretence of restoring the said lace, without apprehending and prosecuting the felon who stole the property. On the day before his trial was to take place, he distributed among the jurymen and others some printed papers, under the title of 'A List of Persons discovered, apprehended, and convicted of several Robberies on the Highway; and also for Burglary and Housebreaking; and also for returning from Transportation: by Jonathan Wild.' This contained the names of thirty-five people convicted of robbing on the highway, twenty-two of housebreaking, and ten who had returned from transportation. To it was annexed the following:

> Several others have been also convicted for the like crimes, but, remembering not the persons' names who had been robbed, I omit the criminals' names.
>
> Please to observe that several others have been also convicted for shop-lifting, picking of pockets, &c., by the female sex, which are capital crimes, and which are too tedious to be inserted here, and the prosecutors not willing of being exposed.
>
> In regard, therefore, of the numbers above convicted, some, that have yet escaped justice, are endeavouring to take away the life of the said JONATHAN WILD.

This plan was a failure. He had hoped it would convince the court of his public service as a thief-catcher. Instead he merely demonstrated to his accusers what a callous individual at heart he really was, content to implicate others while trying to save his own miserable skin.

When he was put to the bar, he requested that the witnesses might be examined separately, and this was granted. Henry Kelly deposed that under the prisoner's direction he and Margaret Murphy had gone together to the prosecutor's shop, with the pretence of buying some lace. He stole a tin box, and gave it to Murphy in order to deliver to Wild, who was waiting in the street to receive their booty, ready to try and rescue them if they should be taken into custody. They then returned together to Wild's house, where the box was opened and found to contain eleven pieces of lace. Wild said he could afford to give no more than five guineas, as he would only get ten guineas at the most for returning the goods to the owner. Kelly received three guineas and a crown as his share, and Murphy was given the remaining two guineas. Margaret Murphy was the next to be sworn, and her evidence corresponded in every detail with that given by Kelly.

Catherine Stretham, the elder, told the court that between 3 and 4 p.m. on 22 January, a man and woman came to her house, pretending they wanted to purchase some lace. She showed them two or three parcels, but they were dissatisfied with the quality and price. They left the shop, and a few minutes later she found some of her lace was gone.

> On the 22nd of January, I had two persons come in to my shop under pretence of buying some lace. They were so difficult that I had none below would please them, so leaving my daughter in the shop, I stepped upstairs and brought down another box. We could not agree about the price, and so they went away together. In about half an hour I missed a tin box of lace that I valued at £50. The same night and the next I went to Jonathan Wild's house; but meeting with him at home, I advertised the lace that I had lost with a reward

of fifteen guineas, and no questions asked. But hearing nothing of it, I went to Jonathan's house again, and then met with him at home. He desired me to give him a description of the persons that I suspected, which I did, as near as I could; and then he told me, that he would make enquiry, and bid me call again in two or three days. I did so, and then he said that he had heard something of my lace, and expected to know more of the matter in a very little time. During this conversation we were joined by a man who said he had reason to suspect that one Kelly, who had been tried for circulating plated shillings, was concerned in stealing the lace.

Jonathan Wild in the condemned cell at Newgate
Gaol, with his account book on his knees

I came to him again on that day he was apprehended (I think it was the 15th of February). I told him that though I had advertised but fifteen guineas reward, yet I would give twenty or twenty-five guineas, rather than not have my goods. Don't be in such a hurry, says Jonathan, I don't know but I may help you to it for less, and if I can I will; the persons that have it are gone out of town. I shall set them to quarrelling about it, and then I shall get it the cheaper. On the 10th of March he sent me word that if I could come to him in Newgate, and bring ten guineas in my pocket, he would help me to the lace. I went, he desired me to call a porter, but I not knowing where to find one, he sent a person who brought one that appeared to be a ticket-porter. The prisoner gave me a letter which he said was sent him as a direction where to go for the lace; but I could not read, and so I delivered it to the porter. Then he desired me to give the porter the ten guineas, or else (he said) the persons who had the lace would not deliver it. I gave the porter the money; he returned, and brought me a box that was sealed up, but not the same that was lost. I opened it and found all my lace but one piece.

Now, Mr Wild, says I, what must you have for your trouble? Not a farthing, says he, not a farthing for me. I don't do these things for worldly interest, but only for the good of poor people that have met with misfortunes. As for the piece of lace that is missing, I hope to get it for you ere long, and I don't know but that I may help you not only to your money again, but to the thief too. And if I can, much good may it do you; and as you are a good woman and a widow, and a Christian, I desire nothing of you but your prayers, and for these I shall be thankful. I have a great many enemies, and God knows what may be the consequence of this imprisonment.

During the four-hour trial the prisoner's counsel observed that in their opinion it was impossible to bring about a legal conviction, because the indictment positively expressed that he stole the lace in the house. The evidence had proved beyond doubt that he was some distance away from the premises when the robbery took place. They conceded that he might be liable to conviction as an accessory before the fact, or guilty of receiving the property, knowing it to be stolen; but still maintained that he could not be deemed guilty of a capital felony unless the indictment declared that he did assist, command, or hire.

In summing up the evidence Lord Raymond, who presided over the trial, observed that the prisoner's guilt was beyond dispute. However; as no similar case was to he found in the lawbooks, it was his duty to act with great caution. He was not perfectly satisfied that the construction urged by the counsel for the crown could be put upon the indictment; and as the life of a fellow-creature was at stake, he recommended the prisoner to the mercy of the jury. They brought in a verdict of Not Guilty.

Wild was then indicted a second time for an offence committed during his confinement in Newgate. As the indictment was being opened by the counsel for the crown, the clause from the 1718 Act was read regarding the receipt of rewards given in respect of receiving or trafficking in stolen goods. The prisoner's counsel argued that as Murphy had deposed that Wild, Kelly, and herself were concerned in the felony, the former could by no means be considered as coming within the description of the Act on which the indictment was founded. The Act in question was not meant to operate against the actual perpetrators of felony, but to subject such persons to punishment as held a correspondence with felons. The prosecution counsel observed that, from the evidence given, no doubt could remain of the prisoner's coming under the meaning of the Act, since it had been proved that he had been involved with felons, and had made no effort to apprehend them.

Having listened to the evidence, the judge said that in his opinion the case of the prisoner, Wild, was clearly within the meaning of the Act. He had plainly maintained a secret correspondence with felons, and received money for restoring stolen goods to the owners. These sums were divided between him and the felons, whom he did not prosecute. This time the jury found him guilty, and Sir William Thomson, Recorder of London, ironically one of the authors of the 1718 Transportation Act, pronounced sentence of death. It was announced that the execution would take place at Tyburn on Monday 24 May 1725. At the same time Robert Harpham, who had been convicted of the treasonable offence of coining, or producing counterfeit coins, and two thieves, Robert Sanford and William Sperry, would also go to the gallows. When Wild was brought up to the bar to receive his sentence he appeared much dejected, and when asked to say whether there was any reason why judgment of death should not be passed on him, he spoke feebly:

My Lord, I hope even in the sad condition in which I stand, I may pretend to some little merit in respect to the service I have done my country, in delivering it from some of the greatest pests with which it was ever troubled. My Lord, I have brought many bold and daring malefactors to just punishment, even at the hazard of my own life, my body being covered with scars I received in these undertakings. I presume, my Lord, to say I have done merit, because at the time the things were done, they were esteemed meritorious by the government; and therefore I hope, my Lord, some compassion may be shown on the score of those services. I submit myself wholly to his Majesty's mercy, and humbly beg a favourable report of my case.

He also said that, had he realised his case was so desperate, he would have prevailed upon one of his powerful friends at Wolverhampton to intercede in his favour. At the same time he thought it not unreasonable to entertain hopes of obtaining a pardon through the interest of some of the dukes, earls, and other persons of high distinction, who had recovered their property through his means. Nevertheless it was pointed out to him that he had been responsible for training a whole school of thieves, and he must realise that he had not enforced the execution of the law from any principle of virtue. On the contrary, he had sacrificed the lives of many of his accomplices in order to provide for his own safety, and to gratify his desire of revenge against those who had incurred his displeasure.

Addressing Wild, Thomson put him in mind of those cautions he had had against going on in those practices rendered capital by Law, made on purpose for preventing that infamous trade of becoming broker for felony, and standing in the middle between the felon and the person injured, in order to receive a premium for redress. When he had properly stated the nature and aggravations of his crime, he exhorted him to make a better use of that small portion of time, which the tenderness of the law of England allowed sinners for repentance, and desired he would remember this admonition though he had slighted others. As to the report he told him, he might depend on Justice, and ought not to hope for any more.

Those who saw Wild at around this time thought he seemed in an unsettled state of mind. When taxed with this, he explained that he was suffering a disorder as a result of the many injuries he had received in apprehending felons, particularly two fractures of his skull, and a wound in his throat after he was attacked by Blake. While awaiting execution he excused himself from attending divine service in the chapel, saying that there were 'many people highly exasperated against him, and therefore he was sure that his devotions would he interrupted by their insulting behaviour'. Moreover he was very weak after fasting for four days. He asked the prison clergy the meaning of the words 'Cursed is every one that hangeth on a tree', and what was the state of the soul immediately after its departure from the body. At this he was advised to direct his attention to matters of more importance, and to repent sincerely of the crimes he had committed. Now that he was under sentence of death, he regretted the escape he had had from death at the hands of Blake, and wished that his former disciple had done a better job, rather than leaving him to meet such an ignominious fate.

He asked if he might be allowed to receive the sacrament, and when this was granted he appeared suitably attentive and devout as he did so. On the eve of his execution he asked whether self-murder could be deemed a crime, since many of the Greeks and Romans, who had put a period to their own lives, were so honourably mentioned by historians. He was informed that the most wise and learned heathens accounted those guilty of the greatest cowardice who had not fortitude sufficient to maintain themselves in the station to which they had been appointed by the providence of Heaven; and that the Christian doctrines condemned suicide in the strongest terms.

While he was in prison he received a letter from a clergyman.

A letter from the Reverend Dr. —— to Mr. Wild in Newgate.

I am very sorry that after a life so spent as yours is notoriously known to have been, you should yet, instead of repenting of your former offences, continue to swell their number even with greater. I pray God that it be not the greatest of all sins, affecting doubts as to a future state, and whether you shall ever be brought to answer for your actions in this life, before a tribunal in that which is to come.

The heathens, it must be owned, could have no certainty as to the immortality of the soul, because they had no immediate revelation; for though the reasons which incline us to the belief of those two points of future existence and future tribulation be as strong as any of the motives are to other points in natural religion, yet as none return from that land of darkness, or escape from the shadow of death to bring news of what passeth in those regions whither all men go, so without a direct revelation from the Almighty no positive knowledge could be had of life in the world to come, which is therefore properly said to be derived to us through Christ Jesus, who in plain terms, and with that authority which confounded his enemies, the Scribes and Pharisees, taught the doctrine of a final judgment, and by affording us the means of grace, raised in us at the same time the hopes of glory.

The arguments, therefore, which might appear sufficient unto the heathens, to justify killing themselves to avoid what they thought greater evils, if they had any force then must have totally lost it now. Indeed, the far greater number of instances which history has transmitted us, show that self-murder, even then, proceeded from the same causes as at present, viz., rage, despair, and disappointment. Wise men in all ages despised it as a mean and despicable flight from evils the soul wanted courage and strength to bear. This has not only been said by philosophers, but even by poets, too; which shows that it appeared a notion, not only rational, but heroic. There are none so timorous, says Martial, but extremity of want may force upon a voluntary death; those few alone are to be accounted brave who can support a life of evil and the pressing load of misery, without having recount to a dagger.

But if there were no more in it than the dispute of which was the most gallant act of the two, to suffer, or die, it would not deserve so much consideration. The matter with you is of far greater importance, it is not how, or in what manner you ought to die in this world, but how you are to expect mercy and happiness in that which is to come. This is your last stake, and all that now can deserve your regard. Even hope is lost as to present life, and if you make use of your reason, it must direct you to turn all your wishes and endeavours towards attaining happiness in a future state. What, then, remains to be examined in respect of this question is whether persons who slay themselves can hope for pardon or happiness in the sentence of that Judge from whom there is no appeal, and whose sentence, as it surpasses all understanding, so is it executed immediately.

If we judge only from reason, it seems that we have no right over a life which we receive not from ourselves, or from our parents, but from the immediate gift of Him who is the Lord thereof, and the Fountain of Being.

To take away our own life, then, is contradicting as far as we are able the Laws of Providence, and that disposition which His wisdom has been pleased to direct. It is as though we pretended to have more knowledge or more power than he; and as to that pretence which is usually made use of, that Life is meant as a blessing, and that therefore when it becomes an evil, we may if we think fit resign it, it is indeed but a mere sophistry. We acknowledge God to be infinite in all perfections, and consequently in wisdom and power; from the latter we receive our existence in this Life, and as to the measure it depends wholly on the former; so that if we from the shallow dictates of our reason contemptuously shorten that term which is appointed us by the Almighty, we thereby contradict all His laws, throw up all right to His promises, and by the very last act we are capable of, put ourselves out of His protection.

This I say is the prospect of the fruits of suicide, looked on with the eye only of natural religion; and the opinion of Christians is unanimous in this respect, that persons who wilfully deprive themselves of life here, involve themselves also in death everlasting. As to your particular case, in which you say 'tis only making choice of one death rather than another, there are also the strongest reasons against it. The Law intends your death, not only for the punishment of your crimes, but as an example to deter others. The Law of God which hath commanded that the magistrates should not bear the sword in vain, hath given power to denounce this sentence against you; but that authority which you would assume, defeats both the law of the land in its intention, and is opposite also unto the Law of God. Add unto all this, the example of our blessed Saviour, who submitted to be hung upon a tree, tho' He had only need of praying to His Father to have sent Him thousands of Angels; yet chose He the death of a thief, that the Will of God, and the sentence even of an unrighteous judge might be satisfied.

Let, then, the testimony of your own reason, your reverence towards God, and the hopes which you ought to have in Jesus Christ, determine you to await with patience the hour of your dissolution, dispose you to fill up the short interval which yet remains with sincere repentance, and enable you to support your sufferings with such a Christian spirit of resignation, as may purchase for you an eternal weight of glory. In the which you shall always be assisted with my Prayers to God.

Neither this letter, nor strict surveillance by his keepers, stopped him from attempting suicide by taking a large dose of laudanum early on the morning of his execution. As he had already been fasting for some time, the only effect it produced was drowsiness. When two of his fellow-prisoners noticed the state he was in they tried to revive him, taking him by the arms and making him walk, which he could not have done alone, as he was suffering severely from gout. After taking a few well-aided steps he became very pale, grew faint, and sweated profusely. Shortly afterwards his stomach discharged most of the laudanum.

A gallows ticket for the execution of Jonathan Wild. The main execution includes emblems of death (left) *and the grave* (right), *surrounded by synbols representing imprisonment*

Henry Fielding, who was then aged eighteen and took his place among the crowds at the execution, was to write a colourful account of the dawning of Wild's last day on earth.

The day now drew nigh when our great man was to exemplify the last and noblest act of greatness by which any hero can signalise himself. This was the day of execution, or consummation, or apotheosis (for it is called by different names), which was to give our hero an opportunity of facing death and damnation, without any fear in his heart, or, at least, without betraying any symptoms of it in his countenance. A completion of greatness which is heartily to be wished to every great man; nothing being more worthy of lamentation than when Fortune, like a lazy poet, winds up her catastrophe awkwardly, and, bestowing too little care on her fifth act, dismisses the hero with a sneaking and private exit, who had in the former part of the drama performed such notable exploits as must promise to every good judge among the spectators a noble, public, and exalted end.

In Fielding's admittedly somewhat ironic judgment, Wild 'had every qualification necessary to form a great man'. He was ingenious, inventive, artful, resolute, and 'entirely free from those low vices of modesty and good-nature'. Not all his contemporaries agreed that he was a great man – merely a great villain. Daniel Defoe's view that Wild's was 'a life of horrid and inimitable wickedness', who sent about 120 men to the gallows for carrying on much the same activities as he was doing himself, undoubtedly came nearer the truth.

Henry Fielding

Wild was still semi-comatose when he was put into the cart and taken to Tyburn. While on his way the crowds shouted out much verbal abuse and pelted him with stones, faeces, decomposing cat and dog corpses and general filth. Daniel Defoe said the crowd was far larger than any they had seen before and that, instead of any commiseration with the condemned, 'wherever he came, there was nothing but hollowing and huzzas, as if it had been upon a triumph.' The public execution of the fallen idol was clearly an occasion for rejoicing.

*Jonathan Wild being pelted by the mob
on his way to execution at Tyburn*

Tickets had been sold in advance for the best vantage points from which to view this most eagerly awaited of executions. Wild was accompanied by Harpham, Sperry and Sanford, who had been condemned at the same time. As he was so heavily drugged, he was the last to die, and unlike them he did not give the customary last speech to the crowds while on the scaffold as he was in no state to do so. On arrival at Tyburn he looked at first sight as if he had recovered from the effects of the laudanum, but he was still very drowsy, and the executioner told him that time would be allowed him for preparing himself for 'the important change that he must soon experience'. He stayed in the cart so long that the crowds were angered by what they thought was the preferential treatment being given him, and they shouted at the executioner to carry out his duty at once, or they would lynch him. The hangman realised that it was in everyone's best interests not to provoke a riot, and as soon as he began to prepare for the execution the popular clamour ceased.

Wild's body was cut down quickly before the surgeons' men could take it away. In accordance with his wishes, at about 2 a.m. next day his remains were interred in St Pancras Churchyard, next to Elizabeth Mann, his third wife, who had died in about 1718. Soon after burial his body was disinterred and sold to the Royal College of Surgeons for dissection. A skeleton thought to be his resurfaced, was donated to the Royal College of Surgeons in 1847 and remains on display in the Hunterian Museum in Lincoln's Inn Fields.

His son had come from Wolverhampton to London shortly before his father's execution. He had a reputation for being violent, and was kept under close surveillance by the authorities while his father was being taken to Tyburn, lest he should try and provoke a disturbance. Shortly afterwards he accepted a financial inducement to go abroad and become a servant in one of the plantations.

Wild's henchman Arnold had been arrested with him on 15 February 1725 and applied for bail on 1 April. This was refused and he was released sometime after Wild's execution. It was rumoured that he had promised or planned to marry Mary Wild, Jonathan's widow, though no records exist as to whether such a marriage took place. With his master dead, Arnold attempted to take up thief-taking on his own account but ran foul of another notorious robber, Edward Burnworth. Both men came face to face at an alehouse in March 1726, at which Arnold was forced to drink brandy and gunpowder at pistol point and was then knocked down. There is no further record of his activities after that, or indeed whether he survived.

Wild's old mentor and rival survived him by two years. Charles Hitchen was caught up in a campaign conducted against 'sodomitical practices' by the Societies for the Reformation of Manners, tried at the Old Bailey in April 1727 for sodomy an attempted sodomy, and acquitted of the first offence but convicted on the second. He had been saved from the gallows but was fined £20 and given six months' imprisonment, his sentence included an hour on the pillory, a frightening prospect for men convicted of homosexual offences, particularly in his case. The newspapers revealed that he had been particularly and 'unnaturally' fond of young men. He was to be pilloried, it was reported, on 26 April 1727 'at Katherine-Street End in the Strand, near the Place where he made his vicious Attacks upon young Youths'. In the process he was badly mauled by the large crowd that came well prepared to torment him, pelted with missiles, stripped of his shirt and breeches, and 'cruelly beaten'. The under-sheriff took him down long before his appointed hour had passed in order to save his life, and he was taken back to Newgate prison to serve out his term. In September, as the six-month sentence was coming to an end, the Board of Aldermen stripped him of his Under City Marshal position on the grounds of his attempted sodomy and failure to perform his duties during the six months he had spent in prison. He died in poverty soon after release, probably from complications and infections from the beating in the pillory and time in captivity. His destitute wife had to appeal for aid from the City Council, and in view of his years of (somewhat debatable) public service she was granted a £20 annuity.

Wild's appearance was described as 'homely to the greatest degree' though it was said 'there was something remarkably villainous in his face, which nature had imprinted in stronger terms than perhaps she ever did upon any other'. Contemporary pamphlets described him as either lame or deformed, though this may have been to enhance and perpetuate the general image of an evil man. If this was the case, it might have been the result of a misapplied salvation, a painful and dangerous mercury-ointment cure for syphilis. One source said that he could put his hip out of joint at will, purely in order to evade the Duke of Marlborough's recruiting officers, who were actively recruiting volunteers for the war against France. The hip socket of the skeleton reputed to be that of Wild reveals no abnormalities. In his youth he had spent part of his time with groups of travelling actors visiting Wolverhampton, and may have learnt from them how to adopt a particularly realistic limp.

Daniel Defoe

For many years, Wild was remembered merely for his life at the centre of organised crime. After his execution the papers were filled with colourful and usually inaccurate accounts of his life, collections of his sayings, and farewell speeches. To later generations, he was more an inspiration to writers and satirists who made great use of his story. John Gay's *The Beggar's Opera* (1728) owed something to his story, and the character of Peachum was modelled largely on him. Henry Fielding's *The Life and Death of Jonathan Wild, the Great* (1743), despite its title is a satirical novel, not true biography. Daniel Defoe's brief account of his life for *Applebee's Journal* in May 1725, and True and Genuine Account of the Life and Actions of the Late Jonathan Wild, are regarded as closer to the truth.

Bibliography

Fielding, Henry, Jonathan Wild, ed. David Nokes, incl. Defoe, Daniel, *The True Life and Genuine Account of the Life and Actions of the late Jonathan Wild*, Penguin, 1982

Hayward, Arthur L. ed, *The Project Gutenberg EBook of Lives Of The Most Remarkable Criminals Who have been Condemned and Executed for Murder, the Highway, Housebreaking, Street Robberies, Coining or other offences*, online, 2004

Howson, Gerald, *Thief-Taker General: Jonathan Wild and the Emergence of Crime and Corruption as a Way of Life in Eighteenth-Century England*, Hutchinson, 1970

Lyons, Frederick, *Jonathan Wild, Prince of Robbers*, Michael Joseph, 1936

Newgate Calendar

Oxford Dictionary of National Biography

Speck, W.A., *The New History of England 6: Stability and Strife*, Edward Arnold, 1977

Treasure, Geoffrey, *Who's Who in History, Vol. IV: England 1714-1789*, Basil Blackwell, 1969